D0195185

"Those who know Isaias Powers or ___ ___ ___ ___ ___ ___ stand that the title of his latest book is just right. Isaias always speaks from the heart and speaks eloquently about the gospel. This book of guided meditations, written in a lively and enticing style, invites its readers into passionate and inspiring prayer, feeding the mind and imagination with the substance of the Scriptures."

Fr. Donald Senior, C.P.
President, Catholic Theological Union
Chicago, IL

"In a very intriguing and colorful style, Isaias Powers brings the reader into close-up encounters with Jesus. His creative phrasing enables the reader to meet Jesus with a casualness and naturalness that is both poignant and effective.

"For example, one notes the title in Chapter 4, 'Bouncing Back,' an expression we've all heard and probably used at some time. But here it refers to those episodes in which Peter so humanly fails and falls in his relationship with Jesus, and how Jesus forever lifts him up. And so it is with the contents of each chapter. The reader studies the plight of the human condition and learns how the compassionate heart of Jesus brings about an uplifting outcome."

Deacon Jerry Christiano
Troy, NY

"Fr. Ike speaks from an understanding heart, and it is our hearts that respond. Gently, through reflection and prayer, he brings us to a greater understanding of ourselves and our relationship with Jesus.

"This unique spiritual guide provides thought-provoking insights on everyday experiences familiar to us all. It invites us to contemplate Jesus with renewed appreciation and to discover the importance of that relationship in our lives. Father Ike explores candidly and with clarity how we think and act in either good or bad ways; free ourselves from compulsions; escape moodiness and depression; avoid worry; and deepen our relationship with Jesus."

Betty Iovine
Human Resources Administrator, Holyoke Hospital

"Fr. Ike has a real knack of standing the world on its head in Chestertonian fashion. How differently we see things, people, events, characters of the gospel, and Jesus, himself, when we look at them standing on our heads. The whimsy of Fr. Ike's writing is never more playful than when he takes a very familiar passage and brings out a strikingly new way of understanding it.

"This book is a gem for anyone who wants to love Christ more and to let themselves be loved by him."

Fr. Timothy Fitzgerald, C.P., S.T.D.
Itinerant Preacher
Pittsburgh, PA

ISAIAS POWERS, C.P.

Heart-Talks
with
JESUS

Guided
Scripture
Meditations

TWENTY-THIRD PUBLICATIONS
Mystic, CT 06355

Twenty-Third Publications
185 Willow Street
P.O. Box 180
Mystic, CT 06355
(860) 536-2611
800-321-0411

© Copyright 1998 Isaias Powers. All rights reserved. No part of this publication may be reproduced in any manner without prior written permission of the publisher. Write to the Permissions Editor.

ISBN 0-89622-722-7
Library of Congress Catalog Card Number 97-61821
Printed in the U.S.A.

Contents

Part II
The Gospel Parables of Jesus, and Us All

Heart-Talks with Jesus

Introduction

Our work of prayer is not so much concerned with getting to know Jesus; it is mostly a question of letting Jesus get to know us. The Lord concludes his Sermon on the Mount with these words:

> Not everyone who says to me "Lord, Lord" shall enter the kingdom of heaven. But those who do the will of my father shall enter the kingdom of heaven. Many will say to me, on that day, "Lord, we prophesied in your name, we worked miracles in your name, we ate and drank in your presence, we heard you teach in our streets..." and I will declare to them, "I never knew you...!"
> —Matthew 7:21; Luke 13:27

So it is with us. We too could say that we know a lot about Christ, but this is not enough. The Lord might say to us, "Yes, you got to know me—but you never allowed me to get to know you."

Throughout the gospels, Jesus insists that he must get to know us better. He earnestly wants to forgive our sins. But first we must admit those sins—and know what they are—and be sorry for them. He also wants to help us improve the good side of our nature. But how can he do this, if we refuse to admit we have good qualities?

The title of this book means what it says, and more than it says. It is a book that can help you find Jesus and learn more about yourself. It is also a book that "comes upon Jesus as he is in the act of discovering you." We open ourselves up to Jesus and he is delighted with the familiarity this kind of friendship brings.

Another advantage of these pages: they will help you discover aspects of Christ's teaching on a more profound level and in a more practical way. You will be surprised as you discover Jesus with fresh eyes.

Our Lord promised that God will welcome all of us people, both good and bad (Matthew 22:1–13). (See the last chapter of this book.) These words do not imply that wicked people as well as the virtuous will enter heaven. All of us are "the good and the bad." We are a mix. At times our personalities display the bad side that crops up in us; at other times we give evidence of our goodness. So, even with our faults, we will be greeted warmly.

But the requisite for entering the realm of perfect happiness is that Jesus should introduce us. The better he knows us, the better he will do his job.

This book contains guided imagery prayers that will help you develop the you-and-Jesus-relationship. From the gospel scenes, you will be taken to a setting where prayer can happen. There, Jesus will talk to you; then you will respond with a prayer from your heart to him.

It is that simple. The rest of the work is up to the Holy Spirit.

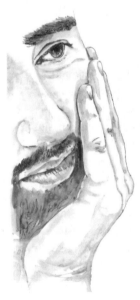

Part I

The Gospel Events of Jesus, and Us All

Most people are good people. I assume you are basically good. You show God, and us all, that you are good...most of the time.

But don't get a big head. When I say good, I refer to only about 70% of who you are. That is, more or less, 70% of the time. In 70% of your situations, more or less, you live your life deserving of Christ's benedictions.

However, there are those situations and moods which must be listed under the heading of your 30% bad side. (This 30% is a general figure. It will vary a few degrees with each individual.) Sometimes you operate out of the mean side of you—that "cranky minority within." Even St. Paul admits to this. In Romans 7:15 he wonders, "What gets into me, at times? I am not doing the good I want to do. And I do wrong things that I really don't want to do!"

We need to admit this mix within ourselves. We need to probe deeper into the dynamics of both sides of our behavior swings. Why is it that we are both good and bad? Wheat and weeds? Dr. Jekyll and Mr. Hyde? Forgiving and hard? Noble and cruel? Sensitive and callous? Kind and mean?

Why are we such a blend of both? And what can we do to improve things? With honest prayer to help us, we need to diagnose why at times we live joyfully and kindly and at peace—full of good feelings and good will. We also need to discover what triggers our frustrations and mean-heartedness, the things that cause our lives to become bitter or lonely or depressed.

The first part of this book presents the goings-on—and the goings-about—of Jesus. We will meet many fascinating people: the apostles, the Pharisees, and the ordinary people of Christ's ministry, all demonstrating good and bad patterns of behavior, qualities we can certainly identify with. Through prayer we can "enter into" those personal events which brought both warnings and blessings from the lips of Jesus. And we can ask him to help us develop, even better, the best that is already in us.

Chapter 1

Starting Off Right

(Luke 9–Christ Begins his Journey)

Now it came to pass, when the days had come for Jesus to be taken up, that he steadfastly set his face to go to Jerusalem and he sent [his disciples as] messengers before him.

They went to a Samaritan town...But [the townspeople] did not receive them...When his disciples James and John saw this, they said, "Lord, will you command that fire come from heaven and consume [those unfriendly] people?"

But he turned and rebuked them, saying, "You do not know what manner of spirit you are [guided by]; the Son of man did not come to destroy lives, but to save them."

And they went to another village.   —Luke 9:51–56

Reflection

The beginning of this book has to do with beginnings of all kinds that we all experience—when we took our first steps as a child, when we went to school, then went from the neighborhood school to the bigger world of high school, then entered the world of higher learning and/or the job that meant our livelihood. After this, we were (or soon will be) ushered into the era of our middle age and then the different challenges of retirement. All our lifetime is the story of "starting out."

Each one of our beginnings is bursting with difficulties. Consider those obstacles Jesus faced as he followed his destiny, the last year of his ministry. There was no turning back. No doubts. No "what ifs." St. Luke indicates as much. He introduces the last half of his gospel with this solemn and somber prelude: The days had come for Jesus to be taken up. So he steadfastly set his face to go to Jerusalem (Luke 9:51).

This statement sounds the bugle for a whole year's worth of events that were as much of a new beginning as was his birth in Bethlehem. During the first two years of his active career, Jesus was a popular hero. He healed all those who asked him to. He drew thousands of people to his side. The crowds were so dense, so "squashing of each other" that his movements became a logistical problem, a traffic hazard:

> A large crowd followed Jesus from Galilee and Judea and from Jerusalem and from Idumea and from beyond the Jordan, a very large crowd, hearing what he was doing, came to him. And he told his disciples to have a small boat in readiness for him, because of the crowd, for they were beginning to throng him [and push him into the sea].   —Mark 3:7–10

That was the era of our Lord's immense popularity. Now comes a different atmosphere—hostility, antagonism, and an erosion of popularity. This year was the time of the "gathering storm." Many groups of powerful people conspired to do all they could to crush both the movement and the spirit of Jesus of Nazareth. All but twelve of his disciples left him. Ordinary people were afraid of being expelled from the synagogue if they went over to him. More and more of Christ's time was taken up responding to his enemies—who acted like a very offensive Senate investigative committee conducted by political leaders who were determined to do him in.

Even as the last year of his life began, Jesus felt the ominous hints of disaster. They were all around him. No sooner had he set out "on the road to Jerusalem" than he and his apostles were denied access into Samaritan territory. There had always been great acrimony between the Samaritans and the Jews. James and John were frustrated in their attempts to buy provisions for the evening meal. The owners of the grocery store refused to let them shop (and, doubtless, insulted them in the bargain; such is the trademark of bigots, everywhere.)

So James and John returned, empty-handed. They were fuming! Their 30% bad side took complete charge of their character. They demanded that Jesus crush the villagers. They pleaded with the Lord to zap them good! They wanted to see a display of power that would one-up the prophet Elijah when he demolished God's enemies centuries before in the same place. "Burn, Lord," the apostles demanded, "At your command let all their houses, children, livestock, and grocery stores burn to a crisp!"

Whew! What passion! And remember, these words came out of the mouths of disciples who had witnessed Jesus' gentle healing and heard his patient words. Such mood swings often happen when we are mistreated by people whom we already hate. Outrage triggers anger, very quickly!

So the Lord was braced with bad news as soon as he began. Probably this scene, at the outskirts of Samaria, was an omen of things to come. "Will people in future generations rebuff me the same way? Will strangers deny me access as these Samaritans just did? Will the world refuse me welcome? And will my own disciples draw more energy from their hatreds than they draw love from my words urging gentle patience?" It is possible that Jesus wondered about such things.

It seems as though all of us go through our perilous beginnings with questions similar to our Lord's. We, too, can experience rejection from strangers or the loss of an easy flow-of-life we were accustomed to. We could suffer financial hardships—sometimes we might not have enough for a good night's meal. Then, too, we can be saddled with angry or arrogant members of our family, or coworkers on the job who urge us to tell people off and destroy anybody who dares to get in our way.

Sometimes, our emotions and fears tempt us to surrender hope and quit the journey too soon. Such inclinations come from our 30% bad side. While such promptings never controlled Jesus, they have, at times, controlled us.

Not always, though. 70% of the time (maybe 80%) we have set our face steadfastly on the way that we should go. And, despite our fears, anger, grumbling at times, and often bitter disappointments, we did continue. We earned our spurs and learned to be more like James and John after Pentecost.

Prayer Setting

Return to the times when you acted like Jesus as he began his new career. Consider those events when you showed yourself to be at your best—when you first learned how to walk, made friends with new kids at school, made decisions in your mature life that turned out to be pretty good, and perhaps when you settled back, with commendable serenity, into your declining years. Think, too, about all the responsibilities you took on and the different groups you began to belong to. Aren't you glad you allowed these achievements to develop?

You know there were fears in you, concerns about how things would turn out. You wondered, "Will I be accepted?" "Can I be my own person and still allow for the give-and-take of friendships?" "What if this happens? What if that happens?" And so on.

As you consider such things, let your imagination take you back to the early part of your life. How were you accepted in high school? How did you hurdle those fears about whether you would belong or not? What about grammar school? Most of all, what about the majestic courage you showed as you took your first two steps?

Pretend now that you are in a warm, comfortable room. You have just rolled out a VCR and you begin to replay all those "starting out successes." When you get to the very first video—the one that records the time you learned to walk—Jesus enters and watches with you...

Jesus Talks to You

Let us pray together, you and I, as we watch you begin to take those first two steps. Oh, you were scared, all right. With your baby way of thinking, it was much safer to crawl than to try to walk. It was more efficient, also. In no time you could visit every room in the house. But try getting from one place to another with just two legs... How could you manage such a stupendous achievement? And what if you fall down and break your nose? And what if your family laughs at your clumsiness? And what if you never learn to do it right?

Such was the beginning of your fears, remember? Even so—even with all those anxieties hovering over you—you set your face stead-fastly toward the waiting arms of your mother and you mastered the most difficult art of walking on your own two legs.

Wasn't it wonderful that you graduated beyond my four-legged creatures? See how well it turned out. You still know how to do it. Aren't you glad you trusted life? Aren't you glad you tried—even though you were very frightened at the same time?

Then came other challenges. Let's remember some of them togeth-er. Bring back to mind how you grew up with, and shared secrets with, friends of each school year. And remember the times you took your first job, and moved to another location, and agreed to share life clos-er with the one (and the ones) you loved. Think of all this good stuff. It is the story of your life at its best.

As we continue on this "video tour" we both can see how strongly you were tempted, at times, to fear the loss of friends, and grieve too long for the loss of prestige, and worry too much about the future's unpredictability. This was all part of your temptation to bottom out and quit on life. Also, you suffered from opposition, as I did. Certain people were bigoted against you and rashly judged you. Some opposed your every move, your every decision on the job. Some dri-vers on the road and shoppers in the mall seem to have been created for the sole purpose of getting you mad! Oh, you have had your ver-sion of violent temper, just as my disciples did as we started our jour-ney to Jerusalem.

Yes, my friend, you occasionally did give in to that 30% mean-spir-ited side of you. But mostly, you met your challenges well. You stayed steadfast; and growth did happen. And I was with you all the time.

Now, after we've gone down memory lane together, let us pray about the beginnings you will experience in your future. You will be able to trust in life (and trust in everlasting life, with me) as long as you control the negative side of your temper and the demoralizing side of your fears. Keep developing the courage and patience you have so ably demonstrated, in so many ways, so far.

Let us, together, set our face toward that Jerusalem which is in store for you. With my grace and my example—plus the confidence you can get from your past successes—I'm sure you will do it right!

You Pray to Jesus

Jesus, my Lord, give me a good start toward all those beginnings that are still in store for me. And stay with me all the way to the end.

You know very well, my Lord, that anger and anxiety sometimes get a stranglehold on me. My fears about the future can push me into a panic very quickly!

Help me to gentle down all my outbursts of emotion. Tell me to "cool it" in the same way you told your first disciples to "cool it" when they acted up. Release me from my fears. Also, I sometimes get so paralyzed by the future's terrifying possibilities, I freeze up with inactivity.

Let me no longer take those dives. I have done many good things with my life so far. I am happy that you brought so many instances of this to my attention. I will learn from the good of my past history, despite my fears and follies...and my sometimes outrageous behavior. I have, for the most part, loved rightly and done well. I think the world is better off for my being here.

Help me continue to live with trust in you...and with confidence in myself. I want you to be glad you have loved me. Created me. Died on the cross for me. With faith in your promises, I wait for (and work for) the day when I shall take my baby steps into the heaven you have opened up for me. To the place where love is limitless. And the forever of perfect happiness goes on and on and on. Amen.

Chapter 2

Making Good Progress
(Mark 5–A Wild Man Calms Down)

Living in the tombs, in the country of Gerasa, was a man with an unclean spirit. No one could any longer bind him, not even with chains...

Constantly, night and day, he was in the tombs and on the mountains, howling and gashing himself with stones...

Then, at Jesus' command, the unclean spirits [who had possessed the man] entered into the herd of swine and two thousand swine rushed down with great violence, and were drowned in the sea...

People went out to see what had happened. They came to Jesus and when they saw the man who used to have a mob of demons in him, sitting there, clothed, and in his right mind, they were afraid...

Then, as Jesus was getting into the boat, the man began to entreat him that he might remain [as a disciple of Jesus].

But Jesus did not allow him; he said to the man, "Go home to your relatives and tell them all that the Lord has done for you, and how he has had mercy on you."   —Mark 5:1–20

Reflection

More often than not, the world thinks of humanity's course in terms of plunge, not progress. An accepted declension assumes that we go from good and bad to bad and worse. Tragedies like Othello and Macbeth poignantly dramatize this downward slide. The classic tale of Dr. Jekyll and Mr. Hyde diagnoses how the evil character within Dr. Jekyll (what we are calling here the 30% bad side of us) gradually takes control of his whole personality. He who was mostly good, noble, and generous in the early years of his career was slowly gobbled up by what was, at first, only a minor negative aspect of his personality.

These characters animate a kind of dismal prognosis of how our lives will ultimately end up: the mix of good-and-bad gives way to worse-and-worse. Kindly Dr. Jekyll transforms into the abhorrent Mr. Hyde.

Jesus, however, goes counter to this pathetic flow. His directional internet would have us go from the mix of good-and-bad to the ever-improving profile of good-and-better-all-the-time. In other words, if Jesus wrote that book by Stevenson, the title would be *The Wonderful Tale of Mr. Hyde Worked on by Grace until He Turns into the Good Dr. Jekyll.*

In a sense, Jesus has already written that book. He inspired St. Mark to portray the marvelous transformation that came over the Gerasene Demoniac. The man who lived in the tombs was a slave to his own violent, self-destructive nature. He was a hermit of his own hatreds. The beginning of the gospel story delineates a most gruesome "Mr. Hyde." It also hints at the bad side that is in us all whenever we are controlled by the mood of spitefulness toward others and bitterness toward ourselves.

So we meet that man in the repulsive tombs, rejected by the townspeople, hateful to himself. Then he confronts the healing power of Christ. Notice the Lord's procedure. He does not lecture the man. There is nothing even close to a bawling out. Jesus delivers no speeches, such as "How could you sink so low? Where did your parents go wrong in your upbringing? Do you realize what a burden you are to the whole community?" Nothing like that.

Jesus addressed the bad attitudes within the man rather than addressing the man himself. He released him from his howling and hurts. Christ's gentle compassion mellowed the man into his right mind again. The caveman settled down and finally was able to welcome the healing ways of Jesus. He who had been supercharged by every kind of antisocial behavior was sitting down in Christ's company, fully clothed, liberated from all his woes, ready and willing to become a disciple of the love that had so changed him.

The last we see of him, he has indeed become a disciple. This desperado, who for years had refused the company of everyone, now agreed to take on a most arduous commission of socialization. He traveled the ten cities, east of the Jordan River, and prepared all the inhabitants for Christ's visitation.

Prayer Setting

Imagine yourself sitting by your kitchen table at home. Jesus has been waiting for you. You've had a very bad day. The demands of thoughtless individuals have drained you. News on the radio and reports from your network of gossips have swiftly disrupted your peace of mind. Some members of your family have also posed ominous threats to your composure. Offensive drivers on the road have bugged you even more than usual. (Of course, this same disruptive behavior could have come from the pushy people on the subway, bus, or train.) All of these misery-laden situations are messing up your life.

As you sit down for supper, let imagination combine about ten of your worst days. Think of your mood as they were going on. You may never have allowed yourself to get so deep-down into depression that you could change places with that Gerasene Demoniac. You may never have run away into some cave, or drawn blood by thrusting pointy rocks into your own body.

Maybe not that bad. But there have been times when you sulked as completely as you knew how to. You refused to speak to this one or that one; and maybe you even did violence to yourself with drugs or drink or pills or reckless driving.

Muster those circumstances into your mind once more. Mutter and grumble against the world the way you do when you are upset. Then let yourself be startled as you become aware of Jesus in the room. He has been there all the time. But in the mood you were in, you didn't notice him before.

Now you do notice him. Let him be really present to you. He is not about to lecture you. He does not even look cross or disappointed. He invites you to relax... Breathe in and out easily and slowly... Sigh out loud one or two times... Unstrangle the hold that tension has on you... And just listen for a while. It is such a relief to know that you don't have to "explain things" to anyone. Jesus speaks to you in a low-key, conversational tone…

Jesus Talks to You

Yes, life is hard sometimes. I never promised "easy." You remember some of those bad days. Know that there were others you can't remember that were even worse. There were times you wanted to quit on everybody and everything. You've had your version of sinking down into some dismal tomb, festering your old wounds with bitter thoughts and feelings. And sometimes you even dramatized your disgust with life by exploding with hostility toward others or yourself.

On those occasions, the mean-spirited part of your personality took over. But I stayed with you through all the terrors. I have treated you in the same way I healed that man in the gospel who was brutalizing himself because of all his bitterness. Remember, I did not bawl him out for his bad behavior. I challenged the devils-of-discouragement that possessed him. I had more power than a whole legion of those monsters. So I evicted them and put the man at peace.

Once the devils left him, he was healthy again. He was strong, open-eyed, and alive to the best that was in him. He was no longer naked to his enemies or powerless to improve himself. Now he was clothed and in his right mind.

And you know something? That man was able to learn from his bad experience and bring good out of it. When I sent him forth to be my missionary, he was marvelously patient with other people. He had true compassion for the weaknesses of others, real understanding of their angry outbursts. He was able to heal them because he remembered his own bouts with those bad moods. There was a conviction in the words he spoke; he had been there! Hope was a palpable commodity of his character because he had learned to live with the new life I gave him. And he learned. By experience. How terrible it was to live without hope. It was not in some barren classroom that he learned those lessons. It was in a cave—his own.

You've already begun meditating, as soon as you connected yourself to the man in my gospel. Now, I want you to return to those feelings you had when you were experiencing the bad days—when certain people and events brought on your negative behavior, your own version of being "in the tombs."

Realize how desperate your situation would have been if you were the only one you could rely on. You might have lost it all; you might have been a hermit to your hurts. Forever. This malignant desperation could have increased until a whole legion of bad attitudes prevailed.

But you were not alone. I was in your corner all the time. It was I who nudged good people to come into your life at just the right time. I arranged all those "lucky" circumstances that helped change your moods. I gave you my sacraments to heal you into wholeness... And I let you live long enough for the healing process to take shape.

Now, in your imagination, go up to your bathroom and take a shower. Wash your troubles right out of your hair. Let all that life-degrading energy rinse away from your skin. Then, slowly and luxuriously, put on your best clothes—your lucky clothes—the favorite dress or suit or shoes, whatever. Let this outfit represent your change to the better. Let it be your version of "being clothed and in your right mind."

After that, come back to the kitchen where I'll be waiting for you. I have some last words of advice. Some future prospects have been saved up for you. They will be your version of the commission I gave my friend in the gospel. You will hear me say (somehow), "Return to your places of work and recreation, return to your family and friends—and to the new friends I will send your way—and tell them about the goodness I have given you."

I don't want you to be pushy or obnoxious. Don't even think of advertising this ministry. Just be yourself; and be alert to possibilities. Don't worry. My providence will put people in your life—people I want you to help. Because you have suffered, you will understand their suffering. You will be compassionate. You will know the right thing to say, the right way to be present to them. And I will be with you. All the time.

You Pray to Jesus

My Lord, thank you very much for getting me back where I belong. I was tired of those tombs. I was fed up with grumbling at others and gashing at myself and refusing the courtesies of love. It is better now that I am calm and not mean-spirited. It's more worthy of me to be an encourager of others than to stay sullen and snarling at my world.

Keep close to me, my Lord. No telling when that bad side of me will rear up and throw me back into those old caves of depression. Guide me in gentleness. Teach me patience with myself; and counsel me in the right ways to care for others. You don't have to instruct me about compassion. Compassion I already have—when mine was grafted onto yours. Amen.

Chapter 3

Understanding Death

(John 11–Jesus Grieves for his Friend Lazarus)

Jesus said to Martha, "Lazarus [your dead brother] shall rise."
Martha said to him, "I know that he will rise, on the last day."

Jesus said to her, "I am the resurrection and the life. Whoever believes in me, even if he dies, shall live…"

Then Mary of Bethany came to where Jesus was, and she said, "Lord, if you had been here, my brother would not have died."

When Jesus saw her weeping, he groaned in spirit and was troubled [was "angry at death"]. And Jesus broke into silent tears.

The crowd then said, "See how Jesus loved him." But some of them said, "Could not he who opened the eyes of the blind, have seen to it that this man should not die?"

Jesus again broke into tears…

And he said, "Take away the stone."

Martha said, "Lord, by this time he is already decayed, for he is dead four days."

Jesus said to her, "Have I not told you that if you believe, you shall behold the glory of God?"

They then removed the stone…And at once he who had been dead came forth from the tomb.   —*John 11:1–44*

Reflection

More than anything, the fact of death took number one priority in Christ's concerns—the inescapability of death, the struggle of life against death, and the God-given promise of a new life that comes after death. Indeed, most of our Lord's working hours were filled with his battle against the great adversary—our mortality.

No one can doubt that Jesus took death very seriously. Consider the events that happened at Bethany, just a few days before Holy Week. The scenario was a "dress rehearsal" preparing us for the significance of the passion, death, and resurrection of the Lord. Besides Jesus and his apostles, the scene included Martha, Mary, their dead-then-raised-up brother, Lazarus; there was also an impressive crowd of friends, townsfolk, and associates of the deceased.

On one side of this assembly must be placed the majority of the mourners. Lazarus was young, probably in his thirties, so the friends and neighbors hated death for taking him. And they hated God for letting it happen. And they were prepared to silence anybody who told them any of that "pie in the sky" stuff about the possibilities of an afterlife. And they certainly were prepared to second-guess, criticize, and condemn anybody who "could have caused a healing—if he had arrived on time, if he had not dilly-dallied on the other side of Lake Galilee until it was too late!"

"Oh, yes," they said, with undisguised sarcasm, "Jesus loved Lazarus so much! But he helped others. He brought strangers to health who were close to death's door. Could he not have done as much for his friend? If he loved Lazarus so much, why didn't he get here sooner?"

With words like these, the crowd sentenced Jesus—their verdict was hypocrisy. They saw the healer from Nazareth overcome with tears. Some of them understood that he wept because he hated death and he loved Lazarus so much. But most of the crowd reacted with contempt. They went as far as calling him a phony for his display of tears. Martha and Mary were also stricken with sadness. They missed their brother very much. But their grief was not the kind that stormed against God for permitting the death of their dear one. They did not utter public outcries against God...or against Jesus for not being present at the bedside.

Prayer Setting

In your imagination revisit a wake or a funeral that were part of the goodbye ceremonies for someone you loved. Try to recall your thoughts about them—how you miss them, where you think they are now, what your judgment is about God for letting them die...things like that.

Remain in one of the funeral parlors, all alone. Sit down on one of those uncomfortable benches and stare into the space of your own thoughts. Then Jesus comes and sits beside you. His look is serene, a look of tender understanding. He wants to talk to you about death, about your mixed feelings, and about your faith.

Jesus Talks to You

Yes, my friend, I know you very well. I have been inside your soul when you expressed your dismay at the way I run things. You even questioned my mercy, wondering if God existed because he didn't seem to care how terrible it was that death took away the ones you loved.

Don't be embarrassed. I've heard the complaints before, from almost all my friends. Second-guessing God did not begin with you or your contemporaries. All the centuries have engaged in this activity.

Consider the timing of the miracle, when I raised Lazarus from the dead. I deliberately stayed away from his sickbed. Sure, I could have cured him, if I arrived a few days earlier. If I had, he would not have died so young. But eventually he would have died! At some point in time Lazarus would have ceased to breathe. Then what?

I chose to do what I did with Lazarus because I wanted to do more than just grant a temporary release for my friend. I wanted to show everybody, for all time, that I am stronger—and longer—than the greatest enemy of all. My disciples had to get ready for the events of Holy Week. So did I. That's why I did what I did for Martha and Mary... and me. By this awesome display of my power, I proved, ahead of time, that life is superior to non-life—that my promise of eternity cancels out the gloom of the doom of nothingness.

Soon I would be handed over to be crucified. So I needed to do what I did for Lazarus. It was to help me, too. I needed to see the purpose, and the outcome, of Holy Week—the three-step drama of death to life to everlasting joy. This was my destiny, shaping up before me. Now it is the marvelous destiny of everyone.

So now you know, my friend, why the gospel of St. John and the early church put such a significance on the way—and the why—I raised Lazarus from his grave. I did not become human and die on the cross in order to alleviate some of the hardships and handicaps that people have. My purpose for coming into this world was not to postpone Lazarus' funeral for a few years. My purpose was to enter everybody into a glorious life that will never cease.

God sent me to love all people born into the world, and to stretch this love to the non-limits of forever. The life I gave Lazarus was life-from-the-dead. It is the same life I will give you when you die. My love is a love that literally never quits. Never. And it is much fuller, wiser, happier, and more contented than the best moments of the life you have lived so far.

When those you love face death—and you face it with them—you have to grieve for them. Grieve for yourself as well, because you miss them. I grieved, too, when Lazarus was in the tomb. So I know how you feel and how deeply it affects you.

Sometimes you also feel the need to grieve profoundly as you face all those "little deaths" that come your way—things like losing your job, being jilted by one you loved, having a member of your family sever all relationship with you, being snubbed by friends, or faced with serious disasters or bad luck. These experiences are first cousins to death itself. Even the termination of one's normal routine, because of retirement or rehabilitation, can cause a person to wonder, "What's the meaning of life, if these are the kinds of things that can happen to you?"

It's okay to feel this way at times. Sadness in the heart and dismay in the mind are honest reactions. But don't let them have the last word. That's the important thing. Toward all your deaths, grieve the way Martha and Mary grieved—all the time hanging on to hope in me and faith in my promise of life.

You Pray to Jesus

Jesus, my Lord, let Lazarus be the "dress rehearsal" for my resurrection, too. When I face the prospect of death, I will be afraid, because all the things I've grown accustomed to will go away—my speech, my memory, my thoughts, my breath. But hope won't leave me. Neither will my faith. And love can't leave me, because it was your gift to start with. And life can't leave me because, after I die to this world, you promised you would raise me up to yours. I believe that you can do this for me, Lord. I believe as Martha and Mary did. And I trust your love that wants to. When the time comes, let me be passive, as prayer is passive. Let me simply wait for power to lift me up.

But in the lesser deaths of mine, make sure that I am more active in my cooperation with the destiny you have for me. I must do all that I can to help elevate myself from those depressions of mine. Lord, you no more want me to stay in any of my "graves" than you wanted Lazarus to stay in his. Give me the courage that comes from trust in you—and the stamina that comes from faith in you—so that I can rise above that part of me which gets so easily dejected.

One more thing, Lord. Help me to have healthy reactions to everything surrounding the deaths of other people. Let me never assume that I know all the answers, or that I'm in a position to judge anybody who did or didn't get to the wake or come to the funeral. Let me leave in your good hands the ways you respect everybody's free will. We all have our own unique style of mourning. Help me with mine, Jesus. Help me to make it healthy and hopeful. And help me to have compassion for all who grieve the loss of life. Amen.

Chapter 4

Bouncing Back

(Matthew 16–Christ's Patience with Simon Peter)

Jesus began to ask his disciples, "Who do people say that I am?" They said, "Some say you are John the Baptist; others say you are Elijah; while others say you are Jeremiah or one of the other prophets."

Then Jesus said to them, "But you—who do you say that I am?" Simon Peter answered, "You are the Christ, the son of the Living God!" Jesus then said, "Blessed are you Simon…for flesh and blood has not revealed this to you; it was my Father in heaven who did so!"

Then [soon after this declaration] Jesus began to tell his disciples that he must go to Jerusalem and suffer many things…and be put to death, and, on the third day, rise again.

Peter, taking him aside, began to chide Jesus, saying, "Far be it from you, Lord. This should never happen to you!"

Jesus then turned and said to Peter: "Get behind me, you 'Satan'! You are a snare in my path. You do not think the way God thinks; you think the way men think."

—*Matthew 16:13–19*

Reflection

The most likely candidate in the gospels for illustrating how people are more or less 70% good and 30% bad is Simon Peter. The gospels show him drifting back and forth so often. One minute he was heroic, noble, insightful—exhibiting the very best qualities of leadership. Indeed, the Lord himself praises him as "tops in his class," the "Kingpin of the Church!" The next minute he was a snare, trying to prevent the course of love that was Christ's destiny. Jesus not only called Peter "The Rock," he also called him "Satan."

It is good to learn about this magnificent associate of Jesus in all his engaging humanness. Along with his courage and insights and generosity of spirit, Peter did have a tendency to be arrogant and impulsive. This got him in trouble. So often, after a good beginning, he tripped up, suddenly letting panic overcome his faith. Once he saw Jesus walking on the water. He cried out, "Me, too, Lord. Let me join you." Jesus allowed it. Peter took his first few steps, demonstrating great faith. But then he looked down on the raging sea, and fear overtook him. He sank...after he had started out so well (Matthew 14).

The same sinking feeling occurred on the morning when Jesus conducted his informal group therapy session. Jesus asked them all, "What do you really think of me? What is the name that people will associate me with? What will I be called?" Peter, and Peter alone, was given the inspiration to speak up. His response was short and straight, to the point and poignant: "Thou art the Christ, the promised one of Israel and the unique Son of God!"

Wow! Jesus immediately gave Peter a heartwarming endorsement for his insight. He also gave him a nickname, a name that never left him: "Right on, Rocky!" Jesus said. (The name Petros means Rock.) "On the Rock, which you are, I will build my church, which will last to the end of the world!"

This was Christ's magnificent praise for his good friend and top disciple. Then, after only a few minutes, Peter sank back into his 30% bad side. Jesus began to tell his disciples that soon he would undergo degradation, passion, and death. "Rocky" could not abide such a project. He did everything he could to dissuade his master from any hint of suffering or apparent failure. Because of his argumentativeness and know-it-all arrogance, Jesus severely rebuked his friend. Only minutes before, the man was praised for "thinking the way God thinks; not the way men think." Now the Lord changes things around. Peter was criticized because he "thought the way men think and forgot already the way God thinks!"

So went the swing in the life of Saint Peter. He was good and bad, then he was bad and good, then he showed himself to be good and bad again. So like us all.

Prayer Setting

Visualize yourself at your kitchen table, all alone. You know that Jesus will soon visit you; but today you are dreading the encounter. The reason for this is that you have just remembered some occasion when you lived out of your bad side. Your sins were probably like the sins of Simon Peter. Maybe you were too rash or impetuous—thinking yourself stronger (or wiser, or more capable) than you really were. Maybe you surrendered to panic because you feared somebody's disapproval. Maybe it was harsh words that broke off a friendship, or impudent comments that got you in trouble on the job. Maybe it was something else...

Such is the case with all humans, now and then. Stew over your own personal sinfulness for a while. Like Peter, are you abashed by the memory? Do you wonder, "What will Jesus think of me? How can he ever trust me after the weaknesses I've shown?"

The Lord enters the kitchen. Slowly he gets a cup of coffee. He stirs the cup. Sits down. Looks at you. Then he begins to speak in a most kindly way...

Jesus Talks to You

I know all about your wrongdoings and your impulsiveness. Don't stay with the sadness of your guilt too long. Remember Simon Peter. Once he walked on the water, full of trust. Then he filled with fear and sank into the sea. But he did not drown! Don't forget that last scene. I pulled him up, dried him off, warned him about letting his bad side get the better of him, and set him back up at the pilot's chair of the fishing boat.

This was my way with Peter. It's my way with you, also. Consider my friend's most well-recorded sin. The morning of Good Friday, he lied—he swore an oath that he was a stranger to me. I knew he would let me down. I also knew that, thanks to my prayer for him, the strength and compassion growing out of his weakness would be the very power source of all those great qualities for leadership that he would grow into.

When I met with the apostles on Easter Sunday, I did not want them to grovel with shame, or to focus on their past faults. I forgave Peter and the others. I gave them peace. After forgiveness came their new assignment. Supplied with the courage of my confidence, they accepted their commission in the same good spirit that I did, years before. I told them, "As the Father has sent me, I send you." They agreed to all the demands that this send-off placed on their shoulders. And off they went to change the world—full of joy, full of confidence. I was so proud of them. I still am proud of them.

My love-style is the same now as it was then. It is the same for you as it was for my first disciples. Remember how I forgave Peter and the others. I freed them from their 30% bad side. I sent them forth to operate out of their goodness. And they did. My patience and mercy worked well.

Another thing. Remember what happened a few weeks after Easter, up in Galilee? The apostles and I enjoyed a picnic breakfast. Afterward, I asked, three times, "Simon Peter, do you love me?" I was not trying to make my friend squirm by this interrogation; I was not forcing Peter to make up for his threefold denial by a threefold pledge of allegiance.

There was never any doubt in my mind about Peter's love for me. Even when he sinned, he still loved, deep down. No, I kept probing and probing until I got the right response. The third reply was what I was looking for when he said, "Lord, you know all things. You know that I love you!"

That was what I wanted from him. At last, Peter stopped being miserable about himself, about how he let me down and had denied me. He finally cleared away his guilt and admitted what was good for me to hear—and good for him to say—how much he really loved me. By the way I accepted him, he knew how much I loved him, too.

Once this was settled, I was able to tell him the purpose of my questions. In a threefold way, I told him to feed my sheep, to "care for all my little ones." I wanted the Rock, upon which I would build my Church, to love everyone with the same devotion and dedication that he showed when he loved me (John 21:15–17).

This is how things went with Simon Peter. And this is how it will always go with you. Of course, your gifts and responsibilities are different. But your sins are about the same as his. And your love for me is noble, just about as good as his was. Also, you need my encouragement no less than he did. Be assured, always, that I will be with you as closely and as confidently as I was with the apostles, as I am with all my friends.

You Pray to Jesus

Jesus, my Lord, I have a couple of favorite sulking corners where I close myself up against the world and brood about what's wrong with me. You could call these places of mine a personal version of the upper room—the place where Peter and the other apostles were locked into their own fears.

You know there have been times when I too let you down and let myself down and failed others. Sometimes I wondered if anyone (and especially you) could love me.

It is at these times, when I am locked into moods, that I must remember how kindly you treated Peter after he displayed his 30% bad side. You forgave him; you gave him confidence again. That's how you treat me too. You have celebrated your mercy with me already, many times.

Lord, let me remember this when I am down. And let me remember, as I come out of the downspin, how often you have praised me for my good instincts and my faithful prayer and for those times when I was kind to others. As I draw from the best side of my personality, let me hear you asking me, more than once, "Do you love me?"

And give me the courage to admit—despite all my failings of the past—yes, Lord. You know that I love you. Then let me go deep into a silence that waits for the whisper of your Holy Spirit. In this hushed mood, which permits your love to hold me, let me hear you tell me to love others with the love-style learned from you. To feed your sheep. Care for your little ones. Love all the people of your world as well as I instinctively love you. Amen.

Chapter 5

Stirring Up a Joyful Spirit

(Luke 10–Disciples Put a Smile on Christ's Face)

The apostle John said to Jesus, "Master, we saw a man, who was not one of us, casting out devils in your name, and we forbade him." But Jesus said, "Do not forbid him, for there is no one who shall work a miracle in my name and then be able to speak ill of me. For they who are not against me are with me."

—*Mark 9:37–39; Luke 9:49–50*

The seventy-two returned to Jesus with great joy, saying, "Lord, even the devils are subject to us in your name." Then Jesus said, "Rejoice...that the spirits of evil are subject to you; but rejoice [even more] because your names are written in the book of life." In that very hour Jesus was filled with joy in the Holy Spirit and he said, "I praise you, Father, Lord of heaven and earth, that you have hidden these things from the wise and prudent, and revealed them to little ones..."

—*Luke 10:17–24*

Reflection

The story of the original mission is meant to be upbeat story for us all. The Lord intends us to go from mean to kind...from competitive to altruistic...from "Everybody looking out for who's doing what!" to "Never mind who's doing it—what good things ought to be done?"

Without doubt, there was a marked improvement among Christ's 72 disciples between the time when he criticized them for their bigotry and the time when he praised them to the highest heavens for their marvelous comportment as they returned from their first trip on the preaching circuit.

Nobody knows exactly how much time elapsed between one event and the other. A good guess would be four months. So the dramatic change from bad to good disciples can be very enlightening for everyone.

St. Luke's gospel beautifully portrays the progress of how it ought to happen to us all. The apostle John (one of the brothers whom Jesus nicknamed "Sons of Thunder") was the catalyst for the first incident, although they were all involved. An unnamed "somebody" was trying to horn in on their work! This "somebody," not belonging to their guild, was healing people! As far as the Twelve were concerned, he was a ministerial scab!

Probably the individual who was silenced was a man who had listened to the words of Jesus and found hope in them. Then, filled with his new-found enthusiasm, he spoke so warmly on the subject of God's goodness that certain people were able to uncoil themselves from their acute state of depression. Then serenity took the place of anxiety and they were healed.

The apostles should have been happy when they heard about these developments. They should have felt good about this surprising extension of Christ's healing ways. They should have! But they did not. They considered the stranger's words and works to be unacceptable. It was an unauthorized assumption of authority. The man had no permission, no license, no backing from them. Therefore, he must be stopped!

Jesus reprimanded the Twelve for their meanness. They were thinking of themselves, their dignity. They did not consider the good works that the stranger had done in Christ's name.

Then notice the change that came over them only four months later. As they returned from their first journey, all they could think about was the good experience they had had. There was no jealousy, one against the other. They did not mope by the side of the road, or get all upset by "the selfishness of some people," just because a few towns refused to welcome them. They shook the dust from their sandals, shrugged their shoulders, let God be the judge of them, and went off to preach in another place. They did what they could for the people who were receptive, and they rejoiced in the doing of it.

A few months back, they would have been obsessed by thoughts of who was going where, and who was goofing off, and who was more successful or more popular. Also, when they were "picky picky personalities," their journey would have been mostly joyless. They would have focused their awareness on what went wrong—"The people who wouldn't listen to me!" "And those who laughed at me, as they threw me out of town!" "And that village that didn't even let me explain things to them!" Boo hoo!

None of this seemed to occur to them, this time. What *did* occur was the wonderful sense of accomplishment because so many people *did* accept them and *did* pay close attention to their message. In no other place of the four gospels do we see such a clear evidence of good feeling, all around. St. Luke says that they "thrilled with joy." Then the record shows that Jesus also thrilled with the spirit of happiness which was so contagious. The word for summing up that afternoon is exuberance. Indeed, exuberant joy, brimming over with happiness, is the only appropriate response when we thank God for the good use of the gifts he gave us. And when we do, Jesus thanks God for the gratitude that we are filled with.

Prayer Setting

You have just come home from a hard day's work. Things went wrong. You brood, in the kitchen, thinking you are alone. As you brood, remember other bad days on the job. Think of occasions when the "wrongness" came out of contention you had with a coworker or your boss. Or your downer might have come from your spirit of competition with somebody: she or he got the promotion or the big break and you got passed over and your ideas went unheeded...and it wasn't fair!

Then, to add to the pressure, you may have suffered home-contention, too. Maybe a member of your family was fussed over for what you accomplished earlier, yet nobody fussed over you. Or maybe somebody else took your ideas and ran with them, and you got no recognition... and it wasn't fair!

Well, there you are, having one of those "attitudes"; then you notice that Jesus is present, over at the other side of the kitchen. He has been there the whole time. He waits for you to speak. Your first impulse is to concentrate on the "what's wrong" aspects of your life, just as the apostles did when they complained about the stranger who worked miracles without proper authority.

Jesus stops you before you sink into that drift of injustices done to you. He wants you to pick up your thoughts and move them to another set of memories...

Jesus Talks to You

Turn away from those self-serving thoughts, my friend. I know it hurts when you have been rejected or refused. That's why I told you to shake the dust from your sandals. You must let go of that tendency you have to judge people. Free yourself from the negative hold others have on you. Wash your hands of them. Go to another circle of friends. Spend more time with those who do like you and want to listen to you.

Do me a favor. To show that you mean business, go over to the kitchen sink and wash your hands. Let the cool, clean water take away all resentment and bitterness caused by your competitiveness.

After you do this, switch channels in your memory. Bring back recollections of some of the good you have accomplished. Indeed, much of your life is filled with evidences of your kind deeds. This is your 70% good side. I know that you seldom invoked my name as you were helping those in need. You simply saw that they could use your help, and you responded. You had compassion for them. You found a way to release them from their downers so they could start life again with fresh enthusiasm. And you were glad you had a hand in it.

Think of these things, as long as it seems good to do so. Then leave me and take a walk for ten minutes or so. As you walk, let yourself be lost in the memory of those good experiences. When you return here, we'll talk about the good you did with the gifts I've given you.

I'll be waiting for you. And we'll conclude our prayer together.

You Pray to Jesus

(This is a quiet, imagery kind of prayer. You imagine the place and the setting. Then let the Holy Spirit guide your thoughts.)

In your imagination, go for a ten-minute walk. You stop on the top of a high hill. You are alone, because you choose to be. It is a beautiful afternoon. As you sit there, you notice two people whom you admire traveling down a path from another hill. These two people in your imagination could be living or dead, saints or heroes. They are people you have always thought a lot of. You have looked up to them—and here they are, close to you. Signal them somehow. Invite them to your quiet place.

Once they are comfortable, tell each of them what it is that you admire so much about them. Praise them in your own words. Notice how courteous they are in the wonderful way they accept your compliments.

Now the conversation turns around. Listen to each one as they, in their turn, praise *you* for having the very same virtues that you so much admired in them. You have demonstrated these qualities of life in ways that are different from their style. But the very things you so liked in them are the things God has blessed you with. As they praise you, give them time to remind you of certain examples in your life when you have exercised these virtues. And make sure you are just as courteous in accepting their compliments as they were in accepting yours.

(Spend as much time as seems good in this prayer setting. Then invite them to accompany you back to your kitchen.)

As you return, notice that the kitchen has become somewhat larger. It is filled with Peter and James and John and all the apostles, and some of your favorite saints. Jesus welcomes your two friends first. Feel the energy of his joy and the strength of his love for them.

Now it is your turn. Tell Jesus some of the stories of your goodness to others. In your own words, tell him especially how you encouraged those who were depressed. You gave new light to those who could only see darkness; you pumped life into those who were out of luck.

Do not tell him of the bad times, your bad scenes. Don't mention your failures or your foolishness. Jesus knows all about them. He has forgiven you. Also, he knows all about those who refused you hospitality. He knows how they rejected you and he has forgiven them as well.

But now is not the time for all those things. Stick to the good stuff. Tell Jesus about the joy you had, when your life seemed to radiate with fullness. Tell the Lord how it was with you when you were at your best.

Make your report in your own words, your own way. Do not elaborate, or "explain," in order to talk yourself down. Like the first disciples, concern yourself with the good that was done, the healing that was achieved, the new energy that was activated, thanks to you. Tell Jesus how glad you were for these accomplishments. Then see him radiate with joy. Somehow, in prayer, you feel his heart extend with pride because of you—his face beam with pleasure. Whether your imagination allows you to actually visualize him or not does not matter. Simply feel his presence and his joy. (Stay with this as long as it seems right.)

Finally, as Jesus prepares to leave, he might have some last words to tell you, maybe some brief instructions about what he wants from you in the future. Let him speak or not speak to you, as he pleases. (Then maybe you could set up a time for future meetings like this. Interesting: the most important person who ever lived is never too busy to meet with you!)

At last you say goodbye. Embrace Jesus in whatever way seems right. And embrace your friends and the apostles also. One by one, they make their way out of the house. Now you are alone. Thank God for whatever happened during this meditation. It may have been insights; it may have been simply a sense of God's presence. It is all gift. Thank him in your own way.

When the prayer is over, and the silence has had its fill, say Amen.

Chapter 6

Putting Work to Prayer
(*Matthew 8–The Centurion Uses his Job to Foster his Faith*)

A certain man [at the healing pool in Jerusalem] had been infirm for 38 years. Jesus said to him, "Do you want to get well?" The sick man answered, "Sir, I have no one to put me in the pool when the water is stirred; while I am trying to get there, another person gets in front of me!" Jesus said to him, "Rise, take up your pallet and walk." And at once the man was cured...Afterwards, Jesus found him in the temple and said to him, "Behold, you are cured. Sin no more, lest something worse happen to you."
—*John 5:1–15*

A centurion begged Jesus, "Lord, my servant is paralyzed and grievously afflicted." Jesus said, "I will come and cure him." But the centurion said, "Lord, I am not worthy that you should enter my house; but only say the word and my servant will be healed. For I, too, am a man subject to authority, and have soldiers subject to me. And I say to one, 'Go,' and he goes; and to another, 'Do this,' and he does it." And Jesus marveled and he said to those who were following him, "Amen I say to you, I have not found such great faith in Israel!"   —*Matthew 8:5–10*

Reflection

Sometimes, when we look into the future, we see only doom and gloom. At other times, however, the road ahead looks bright enough to say that "fate is great!"

This contrast shows one more aspect of our 70%/30% split. While we do enjoy God's gift of a healthy outlook on life *some* of the time, there also is a real danger of getting immersed in anxiety. Our future can be so slippery a thing to foretell that we can quickly let the "doom and gloom detector" take control. When this happens, both trust in God and confidence in ourselves get corroded...then corrupted... then destroyed.

Such despair is wittily diagrammed in a soliloquy given by Lucy in the *Peanuts* cartoon. On the first day of the baseball season, Lucy ambles out to right field. As she goes, she thinks of her own dumb plays on the field, as well as the dismal record of the team Charlie Brown manages. She mumbles, "We've never won a game!" That was the statement of the past record. Then she stares blankly at the future and declares, "We're gonna lose every game we play for the rest of our lives!"

Meanwhile, as she is musing on the likelihood of losing, a simple pop fly arches over her head. Home run. Then Lucy strolls up to the pitcher's mound and says to Charlie Brown, "Sorry, manager, the future got in my eyes!"

That's an insightful analysis. Because she was all caught up in considering the "worst case scenario," she prevented herself from living in the present. Also, and even more importantly, it was the *past* that got in her eyes. Memory, concentrating on what went wrong in her life (never won a game), predicted doom and gloom for the future.

The senior citizen in John's gospel is another case in point. Henceforth, he shall be referred to as "the grouch." This man suffered from the same syndrome as Lucy. Misery made his eyes so dim that he could not really see who Jesus was, or what Jesus wanted to do. He couldn't hear either.

Already the reputation of Jesus from Nazareth was spreading. The grouch must have heard about Christ's power and his compassion. Jesus stood in front of the man and asked him a straightforward question: "Do you want to be healed?"

If we were in the crowd, we would have urged the man to say "Yes!" clearly and simply. We would have presumed that he'd respond with words something like "Wow! You want to heal me, Lord? Great! That's wonderful! Thanks!" At the very least, we would expect to see the man's face light up and his eyes sparkle. At the very, very least, his head could have nodded in agreement.

Nope. None of those things. The old grouch acted like someone had pushed a button, and out poured the same old litany of grievances. Instead of saying yes to Christ's generous offer, he said, "Every time the healing pool is ready to work a miracle, somebody else beats me to it!"

What a miserable old man! For years and years, he griped about how "some young whippersnapper cuts me off so that I am left high and dry!" Apparently, the healing power of the well was limited to one per afternoon. So, for thirty-eight years, he sat on the bench while the more fortunate invalids, or the more pushy ones, got help.

Thirty-eight years is a long time to brood over the unfairness of life. Even so, when the opportunity came for his bad fortune to turn around—and real healing was made available to him—one would have hoped that the frustrations of the past would be given a rest and the man's spirits could gear up for better things to come.

That was not the case. The hurting memories of past misfortunes were the only real thing in his whole life. The healer had to do all the work, without any cooperation from the healee. Of all the people Jesus cured, this man was the most sour. Consequently, he is the only person who is given a stern warning. A few days after, Jesus met the man again and told him, "Yes, you are healed in body. But let your heart be healed as well. Do not keep brooding about the thoughtlessness of other people. Do not let past failures squelch your prospects for a good future. Get a life!"

What a magnificent contrast to the grouch is the soldier in Matthew's gospel. This man looked to the good memories he had. He was a centurion (a "master sergeant," commanding 100 soldiers) in the Roman Legion. He was authentic, trustworthy in his ability to take orders, reliable in his ability to give them. He built up his "scenario of the future" the same way everybody does—basing tomorrows on our remembered yesterdays. The old grouch remembered his daily routine of being upstaged and frustrated. The centurion remembered his daily routine of giving and taking orders and getting things done well.

The soldier's reasoning went this way: "Whenever an order had to be carried out, I did it. I cooperated with others. I followed the dictates and the suggestions of my superior officers. And I issued commands to those under me, knowing the orders would be carried out."

This was the background, providing the reference for the man's trust in Jesus. He knew how plans develop and power is exercised. Using the logic of this everyday achievement, he applied it to the authority of Christ:

Step #1: God's promised Messiah is here. He is the healer who can command physical laws to be suspended in order to show God's compassion.

Step #2: Jesus can make things happen in the world he supervises, just as I can do in my world.

Step #3: So if he wants to, he will perform the healing. Physical laws are on call, ready to obey orders. So I will simply ask him for the favor and wait for his response.

We know the happy ending. The centurion was praised with superlatives. Jesus was as much elated by this man's trust as he was deflated by the bitterness of the old grouch.

We have both these gospel personalities within us. Sometimes we have the faith of the soldier; sometimes we have the snarling negativism of the old man. Jesus is telling each of these personalities of ours to put a lid on the complaining spirit and develop the lively faith demonstrated by the centurion. We are told how Jesus loves the kind of prayer that has a good muscle tone of faith, built up by practical compassion.

Prayer Setting

Pretend you are sitting near the desk that a centurion of the Roman army has allowed you to use. The master sergeant has left you in charge with your thoughts. Following his lead (the story he just told you about how Jesus answered his prayers) you let your considerations center on your "work world"—those places where you earn your living or go to school or do volunteer work or have a part-time job.

Remember how well you have done. For the most part, you were able to adjust to the needs of others, or follow the orders of your supervisors, or cooperate in all those ways that teamwork is called for. Also, you were able to give orders in a way that brought out the best in others. You have been able to get work done and know that it was done well.

Of course, it wasn't always easy. There was the mix of personalities. Some people had an ego that was ten yards wide. Some were so touchy, you had to handle them with kid gloves. Some bosses were very inconsiderate. There was the juggling of compromise between the needs of individual workers and the demands of the task at hand. None of it was easy. But you managed. And you succeeded.

Now, imagine that your guardian angel has taken some of your best days at work and put them on videotape. They are arranged and collated and given the name *Memoirs of a Modern Centurion*.

You and your angel make everything ready, waiting for Jesus to show up. He does, in his own good time. Be hospitable. Make sure he feels at home. Without preliminary comments, the three of you sit down and watch the film. Then our Lord begins...

Jesus Talks to You

That video your angel made is good. I applaud you, no less than I praised the centurion. From memories such as these, you learn to build up trust. Do not live out your days like the old grouch, remembering past disillusionments, failures, and broken promises. That drains your spirit. Dredging up what is wrong with your world will stereotype tomorrow's forecast as "more of the same, but worse!"

That's not the way to live. The right way to proceed into your future is to return to the success you have had at work. Consider your own achievements and the promotions and the confidence people have had in you. Also think about the team accomplishments when you took part in sports, or the band, or drama, or whatever you did that demanded working together. Going over the highlights of your best days will meet me halfway, as you develop your faith in me. From the best that is in you, you can learn that I also have the power to achieve success and show compassion.

My Holy Spirit will always be the most ennobling form of team spirit found anywhere. Count on it.

You Pray to Jesus

Jesus, my Lord, when I need your help, when I look for healing, when I want to be strong as I face the future, let me pattern myself on the life of that Roman centurion you praised so highly. Let me never lower myself down to the level of the old grouch who could only see misery ahead of him because life had treated him so badly.

Grievances are not the way to go. Dismal moods can only lead to doom. I don't want that. I want to be responsible—trustworthy in myself and trusting in you. I want to remember my strengths; then let my own goodness be the measure that helps me understand the healing power and the care I can expect from you.

With your Spirit aiding and improving me, see to it that I fill out as good a report card as I can manage. And from the kindness I give others and the kindness gratefully received from others, let me put more and more faith in your healing ways. Already, just by praying this prayer, I feel the love by which you give me life, and the power by which you restore it back to me. Amen.

Chapter 7

Resisting Discouragement
(Mark 10–The Blind Man at Jericho—No One Squelched Him)

As Jesus was leaving Jericho with his disciples, a sizable crowd followed him. There was a blind beggar, Bartimaeus, sitting by the roadside...He began to call out, "Jesus, Son of David, have pity on me!" Many people were scolding him, sternly ordering him to be quiet. But he shouted all the louder, "Jesus, have pity on me!" Then Jesus stopped and said, "Call him over." So the crowd called the man over. He threw aside his cloak, jumped up and came to Jesus...and said, "I want to see." Moved with compassion, Jesus touched his eyes and immediately he could see. And he became a follower.

> —*Matthew 20:29–34, Mark 10:46–52, Luke 18:35–43*

Reflection

On the road leading up to Jerusalem, Jesus performed the last of his recorded miracles. It was the gift of eyesight given to a man named Bartimaeus. We know his name because he figured prominently in the early church. He did become a "somebody," but when we first meet him he was nobody of any importance—he was an interferer, a "maker of unwanted noise," a "waste of time."

The important concern for us is not his name or any biographical data. Our focus centers on the way Jesus uses this incident to teach us about love. With patience and with firmness, Jesus warns against sticking too strictly to schedules, to our own time frames. Even very good people can sometimes refuse to listen to the needs of other people because of preexisting demands on their time.

To feel the pressure Jesus was under, during the last few weeks of his life, remember that he knew that his earthly career would soon be over. As he left Jericho to go up to Jerusalem, he knew that he would meet with the authorities, spend hours responding to their accusations, prepare for the Passover Supper, and arrange his thoughts for the last words he would say to his disciples. All this still had to be done. Not much time left. His heart already had a hurry in it.

Think of Jesus as a "presidential hopeful," campaigning from one whistlestop to another, on a very tight schedule. He was surrounded by a mob of people, some of whom were well-wishers, some the curious, some the pushy ones asking for favors. His enemies were there, of course, trying to trap him in his words. There were also the "media people" attempting to get a "fix" on him so that they could inform the inquiry board in Jerusalem (and also stir things up for a populace that was already on the brink of revolution). Finally, there were Christ's close disciples who had become quite "antsy" about his gentle ways because they were urging Jesus to spark a political upheaval and start a glorious new dynasty.

Everyone there was energized by their own agenda...as they pushed Jesus along at the head of a large parade. Each individual and each group lobbying for their own special interest—all of them having a different idea of how the wonder-worker ought to use his time.

On the other side of this "pressurizing populace" was Jesus. He was alone in the midst of all this turmoil. Then suddenly, a loud and pesty cry came from a beggar, off on the side of the road. The people were dismayed, annoyed, upset. That obnoxious character had no business interfering with important matters! The people in the crowd, so divided among themselves over what ought to be done, were solidly united about what should not be done. The interloper had no business crying out. He must be silenced, flung back into the ditch, and told to stay there!

Jesus silenced the silencers. He stopped the parade, put all his own priorities on hold, and commanded that the blind man be brought to him. Jesus asked, as he did so often, "What do you want from me?" Bartimaeus had no trouble responding. Immediately he said, "Lord, give me the power to see."

And so it happened. The people marveled. The "Investigation

Committee" was silenced, for a time. And a grateful Bartimaeus was introduced as the newest member of Christ's Apostolic Band.

Prayer Setting

Pretend you are part of that crowd on the dusty road just outside the town of Jericho. In your imagination, take your place beside all the other impatient people who are criticizing the blind man for speaking up. You are helping to push the poor old guy back into the ditch.

Put your memory to work. Think of all those people (within the last year or so) who did things in such a way that you got impatient, or angry, or furious because they interrupted you. Also, think of others who caused you grief because they put unfair demands on your time.

Let all these obnoxious individuals get "immersed" in the one man called Bartimaeus. Now see yourself pushing everybody who irritates you into the ditch. Bawl them out—the same way you usually do—for upsetting you and detaining your plans. Then stand apart from the crowd and fold your arms. Feel satisfied because you have gotten rid of a lot of unwelcome characters who were asking for a lot of bothersome favors.

Then you notice Jesus. He leaves the crowd to fight on their own. He walks over to you. The look on his face suggests bewilderment, puzzlement. Perhaps he sighs, slightly. Then he looks over your shoulder and calls all those people you have just shoved aside. He welcomes them, listens to them intently, loves them well...

Jesus Talks to You

You know I am displeased by the snobbery and spitefulness that comes over you at times. You also know how I dislike that possessiveness about your own time. I have made you aware of it once again. That's enough. This prayer is meant for inspiration. It is not the time for scolding scolders.

I beg you to look longer and to pray more deeply about how I responded to people whenever they asked me for favors. I want you to imitate me in the way I shelved my own priorities whenever somebody like Bartimaeus asked for help.

Of course, there are situations where it is right to say *no* or *not now*.

You can't always be agreeable, in every circumstance, all the time. As you know, I said *no* to people, often. In my three years of ministry, there was no let-up of crowds, jostling me, demanding that I attend to them. Even so, I would often go away from them in order to pray in silence or retreat to some secluded place with my apostles. We did this in order to converse easily with each other and to enjoy our company, without interruption. For, with the crowds of people, there was no leisure for us, even to eat. (See all these passages in St. Mark's gospel: 1:35; 1:45; 3:13; 4:35; 6:30–37, 7:24; 9:30 and 11:11. The best summary is Luke 5:16.)

Sometimes you too must say *no* to people. Sometimes you just need to be alone. Also, you have to relax, on occasion. You need to be with friends, to enjoy a peaceful evening, or go on a vacation that will be restorative.

While this is true, you cannot demand that you be in such command of your own time that you are not able to adapt to unforeseen calls for help. It is understandable that you feel annoyance when people phone and ask your assistance at the worst moment possible. You won't always be serene when the pressure is on and you are already late for this or that. You will suffer from the pressure of so much to do, and not enough time to do it. Yes. I did too. But that's what it means to serve others. Serve them with the gift of time.

Go back to Jericho every now and then. Redefine your importances and develop resilience. Make schedules a little more flexible, so they can absorb shocks in the system. And be ready for surprises. At the most inopportune moments, your journey through life will have to stop, so that you can attend to the needs of *your* version of the blind man crying out for help near Jericho.

Develop an instinct for cordiality whenever these situations come up. Be agreeably accommodating to the needs of others. After all, I came on earth, not to be served by others, but to serve them. Of all the things good people like you must work on is to be more generous in giving that most precious commodity of all—the gift of time.

You Pray to Jesus

Jesus, my Lord, let me put balance in my life. With so many things I must do, day in and day out, and so little time to do them, it's very hard, sometimes, to know when to say yes and when to say no. Let me learn from you, Jesus. Don't let me take my cue from my own moods or the peevishness I can get into. And don't ever let me think that my preplanned agenda is the most important thing in the world. Let me be more of a time-giver, not so much of a time-consumer. You told us, Lord, that where our treasure is, there is our heart, also. Well, my most cherished possession is my own time—especially the time that I dearly want to save for me, myself, and I. Let me put my treasure back into the field of loving-kindness.

Help me to be the gentleness of your voice, my Lord, and the kindliness of your gestures. When people call for my help, let me stop the parade and care for them. I want to include others into your embrace of wholeness and into my embrace of love. Amen.

Chapter 8

Loving "Little Ones"
(Matthew 19–Jesus—Never Too Busy for Anybody)

People were bringing their little children to Jesus so that he could place his hands on them and touch them. But the disciples saw this and they scolded [the parents] sternly. Jesus became indignant when he noticed it. He called for the children and said to his disciples, "Do not shut them off. Let little children come to me, and do not hinder them. The kingdom of God belongs to such as these..." Then he embraced and blessed them, placing his hands on them.   —*Matthew 19:13–15*

Reflection

Once again, Jesus clashes with a bunch of critics. In the last chapter, our Lord scolded those who were scolding the blind beggar at Jericho. Here, in Matthew 19, we are told of another contrast between a kindly Jesus, so affable with his afternoons, and the critical "other people," so absorbed in their own priorities.

The "others," in this case, were the apostles. They were the very best friends of Jesus and the avid students of his teachings. In many cases, they were wonderful disciples. But this time, they flunked. Probably the greatest temptation to sin among good people is in the jealous way we want to control others, and control time. Good people often neglect the good they *could* be doing because of the irritation they feel when something comes up to ruin their schedules or frustrate the plans they have for their family or friends. Even though we are good people, usually, that 30% "cranky minority inside us" can rule the roost whenever plans get scuttled and hopes-for-progress take a setback. It's easy for us to identify with those pushy disciples who demonstrated their nagging disposition one afternoon in the hill country of Galilee.

Oh, they meant well, of course. (So do we all, when we get cranky!) They wanted Jesus to stop wasting time in a region considered to be of no importance. The wealthy and influential citizens lived in the big cities, Jerusalem especially.

So, according to the apostles, Jesus was wasting precious time with these "hillbillies from nowhere." The twelve special disciples had other plans for their master. There were people to meet, leaders of society whose opinions really mattered. There were manifestations of power to engage in—real "eye openers" that would set the world on fire and start the military campaign designed to rout the Roman soldiery, dislodge corrupt officials, and free the people from burdensome taxes. Then they would set up a new Davidic Kingdom which would rival any realm on earth.

Everyone would live happily ever after. Jesus would be king of this realm. The apostles, naturally, would be the cabinet members, the governing body for all practical concerns. The world would love them for their wisdom and respect their influence for good.

Such were their thoughts. But these lofty plans had no room for frivolity or relaxation, or taking time off to bless children and tell them stories to make them laugh—or to bless their parents and tell *them* stories to make them think.

The Lord was quite content to spend his day like this. He refused to allow friends or enemies to steer him another way. Again and again, he told his overeager apostles that the Kingdom he was founding was not going to be "something like Solomon's." It would be made up of little children and the dispossessed and the ordinary people. His preference went to the nobodies; and his afternoon was spent delightfully by telling stories to those who had uncluttered minds and a capacity to listen.

It's good to remember that Jesus seldom scolds anybody. But the one group he always scolds are those who are scolding others.

Prayer Setting

Pretend you have taken the afternoon off. You needed to get away from noise, so you came home early. Prepare a simple lunch for yourself. As you are eating, imagine two groups forming outside your window. They are getting ready to pose for photographs.

One group represents real people in your life, individuals like the parents and children Jesus blessed in Galilee. In your case, they would be all those whom certain friends of yours consider to be "nobodies."

The other group posing for their photo are not real people at all. They are personifications of different aspects of your life. They represent certain things you do—and certain things you think about—during the course of your days. They do not represent the practical or prudent side of you. These are the fun parts of you, the "party and poetry" side. Pretend they are people and imagine what they would look like if they posed for a photograph. What would be the form of that part of your life called your "spirit of prayer?" What would your "leisure moments" look like? How would "daydreaming" appear to you, if it were personified? Would you include "watching a sunset?" "listening to music?" "having fun with children?" (Don't be too rational about this dream sequence. Let a spirit of fun decide how all these representations should look as they jostle for position and kid around with one another.)

Now notice a completely different group standing behind you. These are the critics of your life. Just as it was with Jesus, these people complain that you take up too much time with people they do not consider to be worthwhile and those aspects of your life which they consider wasteful.

Jesus is the photographer. He first welcomes all the "little ones" who have gathered. (They are his friends, too.) He also enjoys talking to the various personalities that are a part of you—your prayerful, creative, and delightful sides. He jokes with them for a while, engages them in small talk, putting all of them at ease.

Then he turns to the "murmuring group" behind you. He tells them to be quiet. He warns them not to interfere.

When he finishes with the camera work, he thanks all the participants, tells your critics to stop being so judgmental, dismisses everybody but you...and settles down to have a little chat...

Jesus Talks to You

My friend, you realize that the group behind you, those whom I called "scolds," are really you. You can sometimes be your own worst enemy, your severest critic. You can get so worried about "What will others think of me?" that you can't be true to your best self.

You let judgmental people worry you too much. You get too upset about schedules. The idea of efficiency should not take on such importance that you lose all your fun and creativity.

Take it easy. Tell more stories. Do some daydreaming. Love my little ones. Notice those in need. Be kinder to yourself. Never stop praying. And care for all those in your life whom I have blessed by my stories and my time.

You Pray to Jesus

Jesus, it is so easy to wrap my life around other people's expectations. It is so tempting to knuckle under this world's pressure. Let me defuse myself. Give me more "Galilee time" with you and with the people that make my life delightful. Let me, by prayer, be like those children in that beautiful gospel scene. I want to come close to you. I want you to bless me and tell me stories and point out the importance of people you have given me and the places you have put me in.

Let me not fuss so much about deadlines and agendas. Let me give priority to *life*lines, not *dead*lines. Let me enjoy the sprightliness of your grace and the kind of life that delights in the love of little ones... and the luxury of sometimes wasting time.

With your help, Lord, I will be happier, and I will show it. Let me be glad to use well all the gifts you have given me. And, now and then, let me enjoy easy afternoons with everybody but "scolds." Amen.

Chapter 9

Keeping a Sense of Humor

(John 9–Faith Gives Us "Bounce Back Ability")

The neighbors said to the man born blind, "How were your eyes opened?" He answered, "The man who is called Jesus made clay and anointed my eyes and told me to go to the pool of Siloam and wash. I went. I washed. I see..."

They then took him to the Pharisees who said to the man, "How did you receive your sight?" The man said to them, "Jesus put clay on my eyes. Then I went and washed; and now I see."

The Pharisees did not believe [all this] until they called the parents of the man and questioned them. His parents answered them, "We know that this is our son; and we know that he was born blind. But how he now sees, we do not know; or who opened his eyes, we do not know. Ask him. He is of age. Let him speak for himself."

These things the parents said because they feared the leaders of their people. It was already decided that if anyone were to confess Jesus to be the Christ, he would be put out of the synagogue. This is why his parents said, "He is of age, ask him."

Then the leaders once again called the man who was blind and said to him, "Give glory to God! We ourselves know that Jesus is a sinner!" The man responded, "Whether or not he is a sinner, I do not know. One thing I do know is that I was blind and now I see. We all know that God does not listen to sinners. But anyone who does God's word will be heard by God. Not from the beginning of the world has it happened that anyone opened the eyes of a man born blind. If Jesus were not from God, he could do nothing." They answered him, "You have been disabled all your life; and do you presume to teach us?" And they turned him out.

Jesus heard that they had turned him out and said to him, "Do you believe in the son of God?" The man said, "Who is he, Lord, that I may believe?" Jesus said, "It is I—I who am speaking to you." The man said, "I believe, Lord!" And falling down, he worshipped him.

—*John 9:1–38*

Reflection

Especially in St. John's gospel, Jesus deals severely with the Pharisees because they prevented truth from taking root in people's hearts. Their basic problem was that they worked for the approval of their own peers and did not think about winning God's approval.

Jesus said to the Pharisees, "How can people like you believe, when you seek praise from one another and do not seek the glory that comes from only God?" (John 5:44).

Their form of peer pressure not only involved the threat of disrespect, it also meant that, if they pledged their faith in Jesus, they would be personally shunned and unceremoniously impeached.

Many believed in Jesus, even among the rulers. But, because of the Pharisees, they did not acknowledge it, for they loved the glory of men more than the glory of God (John 12:42).

The same threat of "becoming a social outcast" trickled down to the ordinary people, too. The parents of the man born blind did not acknowledge that Jesus had healed their son, because they feared the leaders of the people. For already, the Pharisees had agreed that if anyone were to confess Jesus to be the Christ, he should be put out of the synagogue (John 9:22).

In those days, to be put out of the synagogue involved much more than a Rabbi telling somebody not to come to services. It also meant being stripped of all social, financial, familial, and recreational ties. This is why the vast multitude—who originally marveled at the words of Christ and loved him for his cures—abandoned him like the plague as soon as they were told what the stakes were. If they accepted Jesus, they would be silenced, shunned, and scorned throughout the land.

Of all the things that make hatred so powerful, the most devastating was (and still is) the threat of "You must go along with what we say, or else you won't belong!"

In this story of the man born blind, we see quite a contrast between the man born blind and his parents. The parents knuckled under. They did everything in their power not to get involved.

What a difference to their fearfulness is the delightful spontaneity of their son. His reactions to the threatening world were courageous, level-headed, and spiced with a biting sense of humor. This man had every reason to celebrate. He also had a good reason to expect his family to celebrate as well. His parents had been praying for a miracle. Finally, it came. They should have been overwhelmed with happiness. They should have opened up the wine cellar, killed the fatted calf, and made a big fuss over the good fortune of their son. Nope. Nothing at all. Not only was he not thrown a party, he was snubbed by his family and denied access to all that had been a part of his life.

Even so, notice the good spirit (and the irony) with which this man bantered with the Pharisees. He would not allow them to run over him with their scornful putdowns. They called him a "nobody," a "sinner," an "outcast who was ignorant of the law." It can be a frightening experience to be put under investigation this way. But the man stood his ground. He eyeballed those bullies and gave back as good as he got. He even put them on the defensive, throwing the question back at them: "Why do you keep bugging me? Do you want to become his disciples, too?"

He really pushed their buttons. They became infuriated. So then they gave him the full treatment of their scorn, the ultimate social snub—they kicked him out of the synagogue and left him to rot in the limbo of not-belonging.

Socially, the man was friendless and penniless. Good sense tells us that he did not remain this way. Thanks to the last interchange between him and Jesus, we can be assured that he joined the band of disciples. With his good humor, he could fit in anywhere (anywhere, that is, except the world that just expelled him for daring to say that it was Jesus who cured his blindness).

We know he met the Lord again. John's gospel says that he put all his trust (and presumably all the rest of his life) at the service of the man of God who told him to wash. So he went. And he washed. And he saw.

Prayer Setting

Imagine Jesus and you sitting around a table in a warm old-fashioned kitchen (one, perhaps, that gives you good associations from your childhood). The table is set for five.

Three people come in together. The first, the man born blind, has already been noted. Next is Nicodemus, the aristocrat of Jerusalem. He was the only member of the Sanhedrin who insisted that Jesus get a fair hearing. The high council reacted to his plea for justice with taunts and threats and sarcasm:

> Nicodemus spoke up to say, "Since when does our law condemn a man without hearing him and knowing the facts?" They taunted him: "Do you mean to say that you are a Galilean, too? Look it up. You will not find a prophet coming from Galilee!"
>
> —*John 7:50–51*

The final guest is the Samaritan woman at the well of Shechem. Her life was transformed by Jesus. She was healed of her bitterness and envy. She discontinued her scandalous affairs with men. Thanks to her initiative, she helped the whole town restore faith in the Messiah.

Even so, she was still stigmatized by society. Although the townspeople benefitted tremendously because of her intervention, they still did not accept her.

The woman left her water jar and went back to town. She said to the people, "Come and see someone who told me everything I ever did. He must be the Promised One." Many Samaritans from that town believed in him, thanks to what the Samaritan woman said... Then, when Jesus left—after staying with them for two days—they told the woman: "No longer does our faith depend on your story! We have heard for ourselves, and we know, that this really is the Savior of the world" (John 4:25–42). (Note the biting scorn of those last words addressed to the woman by her neighbors.)

Now all five of you arrange yourselves around the table. Jesus says the blessing, breaks the bread, and suggests that you all enjoy the meal. After this informal kind of "eucharist," he tells you why it is good for the five of you to be together this way...

Jesus Talks to You

My friend, the four of us have invited ourselves to your kitchen so that you can be more comfortable with yourself when taunting or ridicule come your way. We want to help you keep living with hope, even when you feel devastated by rejection. It is very difficult to keep up courage under such conditions. We just want you to know that you can count on us. Besides myself, these three friends of mine are about the best counselors I know. They can help you brace up to those cold shoulders you get in life.

The Samaritan woman was terribly hurt by the fact that her neighbors treated her disdainfully, although she helped them out and gave their lives meaning. Even so, they kept on snubbing her and labeling her a sinner because of the things she had done in her past.

Did their reaction get her down? Of course it did. She has a beautiful, sensitive heart, so she was deflated when her neighbors rejected her. And loneliness did take its toll. But she never quit on life. She never blocked off all opportunities for belonging to other circles of friends. After a few months of feeling dismal, she perked up, shook the dust from her sandals, and left that town forever. In the very next town, she *was* accepted. She did a lot of good for people and married well. She and her husband became my disciples after Pentecost. She had a happy life from then on. She still does, in heaven.

It is the same with Nicodemus. He soon became a pillar of my church. Everyone admired his leadership abilities and his gentleness. But he was greatly troubled at the time of the gospel story. You can imagine how he felt. He was a high-ranking member of the most prestigious club in all society. To be part of the Sanhedrin meant that he was a somebody—he had arrived! But then he broke one of the rules of the group. He refused to hate what the majority decided should be hated. He stood for a fair trial.

So they cast him off, made an example of him, threw him out of the club. He grieved for a little while. He missed the "high politics" he used to be part of. He missed the "perks" too. But his God-fearing principles told him he could no longer be a part of their clannishness and prejudices. So he left them and came to be part of our first band of disciples. He has been my good friend—one of my best friends—ever since.

And you already met my charming friend, the man who was born blind. His services are free. He'd like nothing better than to help you cope with bullies.

And remember, my friend, you have me in your corner, too. I had to learn courage the hard way. I didn't win everybody over to me either. I was ostracized by almost all the leaders in my own country. Like the parents of the man born blind, many people abandoned me. They didn't want to leave me. But, because of the financial crunch, they did. I felt bad about it. Once I wept, long and hard, because the people of Jerusalem turned cold shoulders to me. It hurt. Of course it hurt. But it didn't stop me. I lived through that terrible Good Friday morning, when everybody was cursing me to my death. But I didn't stay dead. My father Eastered me. And I have Eastered you.

So here we are, the four of us. You can count on our help to get you over the ruts of your hurt feelings. That 30% bad side within you will tempt you to buckle under the peer pressure. There is comfort and consolation, sometimes, if you give up your principles and join the crowd, be one of the boys, one of the girls, one of the group! And there are situations where you will want to play it safe so that your daily routine will not be inconvenienced.

Don't weaken. I know you to be noble, as worthy of my love as anybody. Your 70% good side has as much guts as Nicodemus. If you suffer because groups threaten you with any kind of disadvantage, remember that I suffered from these same stings, and so have all my friends.

You Pray to Jesus

My Lord, help me to not be afraid of downers. Sometimes these downers come from feeling left out of the life of my own family. They pursue their own needs and preoccupations, and I am stranded. I can easily imagine how sad the man born blind must have felt when his family refused to rejoice with him.

Ask your friend to teach me how to cope when family treats me like that. Teach me how to care and sometimes how not to care. Both. Let me admit how much it saddens me when I am not accepted. And let me appreciate my family and good friends when they have stayed with me. My world has not crumbled just because I can't win 'em all.

Please tell Nicodemus to stay beside me, too. Even from my childhood, I remember when the gang of kids I belonged to didn't want me to hang around with them. It happened a couple more times in my life, too. I wanted to be accepted by some groups that snubbed me. Jesus, ask your friend to stick by me. And let me let Nicodemus show me other worlds, other groups, other joys to share with people somewhere else.

And please, Jesus, let me be helped by that Samaritan woman in your gospel. She was able to continue despite the fact that almost all society resented her. She still survived. More than survived—she thrived! She adapted. She did not allow other people's opinions to devour her basic love for life. I need her resourceful "bounce back ability."

I hope those stalwart friends of yours will always be my friends. They will help me so that I don't falter or cave into any pressure that goads me to be less just, or less gentle, than I should be.

I need your help, too, my Lord. With faith to channel my loneliness, and courage to overcome my sometimes negative feelings, I will stay resolute as your disciple in this world and then be honored as one of your good friends, when I get to the world to come. Amen.

Chapter 10

Learning Gentleness

(Matthew 11–Jesus Makes Himself Available)

Jesus said to his disciples, "You know how those who exercise authority among the Gentiles lord it over them. Their great ones make their importance felt. It cannot be like that with you. You...must serve the needs of all."   —*Matthew 20:25–27*

Jesus said to the crowds: "Come to me, all you who labor and find life burdensome, and I will refresh you. Take up my yoke upon you and learn of me [that is, "enter my school"]. For I am approachable and gentle of heart. And you will find rest for your souls. For my yoke is easy [that is, it fits perfectly] and my burden is light."   —*Matthew 11:28–30*

Reflection

Jesus consistently warned the people of his world (and ours) not to put themselves on a pedestal. In Matthew's gospel, our Lord used the officers and wives of the Roman army to illustrate this aspect of pagan preening. The nobility strutted around, "making their importance felt"—displaying their authority, barking commands at subordinates, threatening swift reprisals to anyone who did not show proper deference.

We can observe the same kind of arrogant conduct in our world today, as well. At times, we too give in to the temptation of "making our importance *felt.*" Whenever we demand special treatment from family or friends, whenever we concentrate on what *we* need and how *we* deserve to be treated, we are using others to serve our own needs.

Another way to misuse power is to threaten people with some form of silent treatment whenever we are displeased by their behavior. Silence is the deadliest (and often the most efficient) method of demanding obedience from others, and serving notice that our desires have priority over everything ("If I don't get this or that, I won't speak to you again!").

Jesus never punished anybody with silence. Nor did he stoop to other methods of social tyranny that are in our arsenal. Even though his enemies were out to get him, Jesus kept trying to change their hearts. He made one approach after another, told one parable after another. He showed his compassion with the sick and downhearted. He manifested mercy in many different ways. But he did not exploit his authority or miraculous powers for his own ends. He never "made his importance felt" by using threats or any form of manipulative techniques.

He went out of his way to say this about himself. In contrast to the high-handed style of the scribes and Pharisees, Jesus' teaching method was "easy access" and "student friendly." His approach to everybody was engaging in its charm and gentle in its discipline.

He never responded to slower learners in a haughty, "putdown" way. He urged his fast learners to speed up even more. Every student who entered the School of Christ was given the particular challenge-to-grow in the measure of the gifts and talents they were given.

When Jesus said, "My yoke is easy and my burden light," he meant, "The burden and responsibilities that I give you are tailor-made to fit just you!" The metaphor comes from the harness on the oxen, as they grind the wheat in the treadmill. In our Lord's time, if the harness was fitted too loosely on the ox, terrible blisters would form. If it was too tight, the animal would choke. But when the yoke was a perfect fit, the animal would be healthy and his work would be well done.

In the same way, Jesus promises us that his providence will put just the right challenge into our day-to-day existence. He does not make life too easy for us. If he did, we would soon be bored and feel that our talents had been shortchanged. On the other hand, if we are challenged beyond our capacity, such an overload would soon lead to discouragement and self-depreciation.

Our Lord gives us the work of love which is just right for every individual. He won't "lord it over us." He doesn't threaten; he inspires. He uses many different stratagems to get us to do good works on the treadmill of our daily lives.

That's the way it always was with Jesus. And always will be. Now we've got to learn better how to let Christ's way with us be the way we are with others.

Prayer Setting

First, imagine that you are a kindergarten teacher in a class full of healthy, wholesome girls and boys. This class represents all the people you love and live with—family, friends, fellow workers, neighbors—those who are close to you in any way.

You love them all. You want to bring out the best that is in them; and design a style of living that will do this. Of course, you know that each one is different—some are more talented in this, others are more talented in that. Like a teacher in a classroom, you measure the challenges of each person according to the individual capacities for receiving such challenges.

Think of your relationship with them, when you are at your best. You don't expect too much from them, nor do you expect too little. You don't drive them so hard that they get overstressed. You don't make things so easy for them that they get bored. There is no taking them for granted, or judging them harshly, or threatening them with the silent treatment if they don't shape up.

You have loved well, and uniquely, all the people that make up the internet of your life. Like Jesus, you have been approachable with them, gentle of heart. You know how to place the yoke of mutual responsibilities in a way that is just right for each one.

That is the good side of you. It is the 70% of you that is Christlike.

It is the you who acts kindly on behalf of others, approaching people in ways that make mutual cooperation easy and mutual benefits enjoyable.

Now swing your imagination around to consider the other side of your personality. Pretend that you are the captain of a ship sailing on the high seas. Your crew consists of people whom you have pushed around. Maybe you physically abused them. Or maybe it was social manipulation—you threatened them with exclusion somehow; or you nagged them; or you criticized their attempts or belittled their achievements. (Add whatever other techniques you use to get your way, to "lord it over others.")

So there you are, a kind of Captain Bligh on a ship that is moving toward more exasperations. As you go about the deck, bawl out this one, threaten that one, pull your rank on others. Use all the tricks you ever tried to register your displeasure.

Then end up in your private cabin. You have spent enough time rehearsing the mean side of you. Don't remain in that downer mood. It is no more helpful for you to scold yourself than it was to have scolded others. Simply tell Jesus that you are sorry for those displays of arrogance. Ask him for advice on how to get back on the right track...and stay there. Ask him to teach you how to be more humble and easy to get along with...

Jesus Speaks to You

I have been talking to you for some time now, my friend. My Spirit has been in your prayer ever since you put imagination into that kindergarten of yours. And my warnings have inspired you during your "Captain Bligh Sequence" as well.

Continue to learn of me. Relate to all the people in your life, your home, your place of work, the stores you shop in, the places where you play sports or exercise—relate to them in the same way I relate to you. You know you can do it. Remember how often you already have.

And don't complain to me because I seem to expect more from you than I do from others. I have enrolled you in my honors course, you know. I *have* to expect more from you. (Anyway, everybody thinks I go easier on others than I do on them. Since time began, people have complained to me how "My burden is heavier than other people's!")

Not so. I fit my challenges, invitations, and expectations according to each individual's ability to suffer, produce, create, and love. No more, no less, for each.

You do the same. Go easy on yourself and on others. Go easier with certain people than you do with others. Each one has a different level of "challenge-ability." And go easier on yourself at certain times of the day and year. Seasons have different moods to them. Learn how to adjust. And above all, stay with the blueprint you have received from me.

That's about it. Stop complaining. Stop lording it over others. Quit putting people down or snubbing people. And get to work.

You Pray to Jesus

Jesus, my Lord, I felt so good when I pretended to be teaching the children. My body could even feel how the best in me was operating. I felt so wise; what I was doing for each of them felt so right. Help me to live this way always.

My body also felt it when I imagined myself as the arrogant captain of that ship. I became queasy when I thought of how I lorded it over others. Looking back at those times, I always seemed to mess things up whenever I played the big shot. I lost wisdom and love; and friends deserted me. Arrogance always ended up making me lonely.

I don't want this to happen anymore. Please, Jesus, take care of me; and take care of my carefulness. Let me serve others as you have served me. Let me be yoked to your life and take all my classes in your school of love.

Then, having learned from you, and having grown to be adept in good works and faithful prayer, I will one day graduate from your school…and be welcomed to the campus of perfect happiness. Amen.

Chapter 11

Giving Attention to Christ's Last Words

(John 14–16–Eight Times Jesus Pleads: Don't Get Discouraged)

A. On Holy Thursday night, Jesus spoke these words to his disciples:

1. Do not let your hearts be troubled. (John 14:1)

2. I will not leave you orphans; I will come to you. (John 14:18)

3. Peace I leave with you; my peace I give to you. Do not let your hearts be troubled, or be afraid. (John 14:27)

4. These things I have spoken to you so that you may not be scandalized... [terrified, heartbroken]. (John 16:1)

5. Because I have spoken to you these things, sorrow has filled your hearts. (John 16:6)

6. Many things I want to say to you, but you cannot bear them now. (John 16:12)

7. You shall be sorrowful, but your sorrow shall be turned to joy. A woman about to give birth is sorrowful because her hour has come. But when she has brought forth her child, joy makes her forget her anguish because life has come into the world... So I shall see you again, and your hearts will rejoice, and your joy no one will take away from you. (John 16:20–22)

8. [The conclusion of Christ's address]: These things I have spoken so that, in me, you may have peace. In the world you will have affliction. But have confidence; I have overcome the world. (John 16:33–34)

9. All these things I have spoken to you so that my joy may

be in you and that your joy may be made full. (John 15:11)

B. Just before he ascended into heaven, Jesus said to his disciples, "I send forth upon you the promise of my Father. But wait here in the city until you are clothed with power from on high." Then he led them out towards Bethany...and he blessed them. And as he blessed them, he parted from them and was carried up into heaven.

And they worshipped him...Then they returned to Jerusalem with great joy; and they were continually praising and blessing God. Amen.

The conclusion of Luke's Gospel.   *—Luke 24:49–53*

Reflection

On the most important evening of his life (and their lives), Jesus tried his very best to cheer up his disciples. It was Holy Thursday. Our Lord told them, "I have really looked forward to this night. Tomorrow, I will be handed over to my enemies and delivered up to my painful death. But that comes later. Right now, I am with you. I have saved up my most important messages for this sacred night. I am preparing to give you my own body and blood. I want you to understand my love for you so that you will love one another in the same way."

This was Christ's fervent wish. But the hearts of his apostles were blocked. He saw the panic on their faces. He sensed their mood of hopelessness. So he shrugged his shoulders, bowed to the inevitable, and then he changed the conversation. As he left his theme of love, he simply said, "I have much to tell you, but you cannot bear it now" (John 16:12).

Then our Lord launched his "Encouragement Campaign." Eight times, in eight different ways, he tried to create a spark of life that would move them away from their mood of doom and gloom. See the montage of texts at the beginning of this chapter, all from St. John's gospel. The Lord tried and tried to urge them to "Please cheer up. Please cheer up! Don't let your hearts be so sad! Don't be troubled or afraid!"

He was not successful. The passion of our Lord began that evening, with Jesus not able to get through to his disciples. Because of the emotional obstacles that had filled their hearts, they proved unequal to the tests of courage. Soon after the Last Supper, they fell asleep, then took flight. Simon Peter denied he even knew Jesus of Nazareth, swearing an oath as he did so.

We can identify with those disconsolate disciples. Sometimes we have let our fears infect all of our consciousness. We have had days when we were so shackled by our agitations, or causes of unrest, we weren't able to think straight, or act just right, or hear any words of hope. It was as though Jesus kept appealing to us not to get discouraged—to please cheer up—but we were already discouraged…and so nobody was "at home" to take the message.

That was the time when the apostles worked out of their bad side. Soon after, though, they experienced an amazing upswing. A mere seven weeks separated the two scenes, but what a world of difference!

On Ascension Thursday, as Jesus was about to leave his disciples for good, he told them to wait—"Wait for power from on high!" That's all he said—be still and wait. If they were sad at heart before, this time they should have been overwhelmed with grief. Jesus was not returning. No longer did he attempt to reason with them (as he had done 42 days before). Now he was brief and to the point.

One would imagine, therefore, that depression would have increased significantly. They would have made a worse scene than they did before. Not so! This time their mood was all *joy*. In a spirit of trusting faith, they returned to their upper room and waited, and were undisturbed.

Isn't that a magnificent turnabout! What was the basis for such a change of heart? What took place that transformed the face of the apostles on Holy Thursday into the face of these same apostles just a few weeks later?

Obviously, something tremendous happened during those intervening weeks. Easter is what happened. The beauty and goodness and power of Jesus finally affixed itself deep in their hearts. Jesus showed them the wounds in his hands and side. They were trophies now of his triumph. He talked to them and ate with them and put their fears to rest.

Instead of concentrating on themselves, their failures, and their worries, what now drew their attention was the way Jesus proved true to all his promises. He overmastered death and showed his power to destroy all of death's subordinate disasters—anxiety, discouragement, despair.

We have the same reason to trust Christ's promises. We are the recipients of the very same love, the same victory. We have also received the same command to wait for power from on high. Our time is after Easter, too. So we must bury that Attitude of Dismay. We receive the same commission to love as the first disciples did. Our version of that hillside near Bethany is the world God put us into.

Prayer Setting

Imagine that you are at home. Today, a festival meal has been prepared. You are the host for Jesus and his apostles. Let your mind, informed by prayer, fill in the time as you enjoy each other's company...

The lunch is over. Let two or three of the apostles tell you about the change of heart that occurred between Holy Thursday and Ascension Thursday. Let St. Peter be the last to speak up. He tells you about how terrible he felt, especially on Good Friday and during those weeks of partial doubt before Pentecost changed him into a new man.

Peter shares some of the concerns that afflicted him—how he was close to despair as he endured those long, long hours before Easter, how he kept wondering "was it worth it?" because it seemed that three years traveling with the Lord got him nothing, how his wife was sick back home, his children were short of food...And there he was, with the others, locked in an unventilated room, afraid for their lives as they heard soldiers shouting in the streets. Then, on the top of all that, the apostles were bickering with one another about what should have been done and who was most at fault and who was the more important... As Peter admits to you, it was all so depressing.

In your imagination, reflect on how often you too have been tempted to quit on life. You also have denied Christ (one way or another) because of something you were going through. At times, you behaved like Peter when you caved in to other people's bullying tactics. You sometimes let envy get in the way of prayer. In fact, your obstacles to growth have been just about the same as those portrayed by the first disciples.

It is good, at times, to admit one's faults. But it is far more helpful to dwell on the 70% good side of you (and the 100% good side of Christ) so that you may draw energy from the after-effects of Easter, rather than linger on the "what's wrongs" of before.

Jesus Talks to You

I know all about your backsliding into discouragement. I know your fears and envious thoughts and all that stuff. I forgive you, just as I forgave my first disciples on Easter Sunday afternoon. I told them to be at peace. I spoke of my confidence in them. I gave them a fresh start on life.

You remember the gentle way I took them back. I didn't bawl them out. I didn't remind them about how they let me down. I never once brought up their sins. I forgave them their sins, concentrating on their good side. And one more time I told them why I chose them to be with me: "As the Father has sent me," I told them, "I send you."

It is the same here. You are forgiven. Be at peace. Die to the worst side of you so that you may live a better life, working out of your goodness. Be rooted in the victory over death I give you.

Wait for more power from on high. Love others as I have loved you. Fare well.

You Pray to Jesus

Come alive to me as I pray to you, my Lord. Help me to settle down. Drive out of my heart all causes for unrest. Speak to me as you did to your apostles.

Train me in the same confidence you gave them. I want to control those fears and hurt feelings which disable me at times. I don't want any spiritual leeches draining my energy. No longer.

I want to hear your words, telling me how you send me forth into my world with the same encouragement with which you commissioned your first disciples. I want to be reminded, over and over, of those three essential commands of yours:

Wait—for Power from on High! Be still—in a Spirit of attentive prayer! Love—as I have loved you!

Let me hear you loud and clear...and often. And let me respond as Blessed Mary did, when she began God's work of love at the Annunciation. She said, "Yes. Let it be done to me, according to your will."

I want to be in your Mother's company, My Lord. I want to say yes, too. Amen.

Part II

The Gospel Parables of Jesus, and Us All

Many of Jesus' parables are designed to contrast the good side of us (and how we can develop it more) and the bad side of us (and how we can control it better).

For instance: A. We are wrong when we sit back and demand that everybody else should put on aprons and wait on us. B. We are right when we put on our own aprons, serve the needs of others... and then patiently wait for Jesus to reward us, at the end of time, when he will put on *his* apron and wait on *us*.

Our work is to control one tendency and develop the others. Nobody has the same degree of good vs. bad. Honest prayer will determine how much emphasis we should give to this or that aspect of our attitudes and behavior. All of the considerations are important. But some will need more attention, a more resolute decision to apply Christ's teaching to our daily lives.

When we better understand both sides of our own makeup, we can repent of our mean behavior patterns by diminishing (or at least controlling) those traits which shame us to ourselves.

And, more importantly, we also can own up to the best that is in us. Thanks to the prayer-sourced encouragement of Jesus, we will be able to see more clearly the occasions when we were patient, peaceful, joyful, caring, encouraging, kind. We can tap these situations and use them to motivate us further, and better, and fuller. Thus we will become more alive to all the aspects of our life, and all the gifts God has given us. And, with the confidence that comes from Christ, we can claim God's pleasure for having created us...and look forward to the joys of his everlasting appreciation.

Chapter 12

Making Sure Things Grow

(Matthew 13–And the Lord Said, "Cool It!")

A. Jesus spoke this parable about patience:

A man sowed good seed, but then an enemy came and sowed weeds among the wheat and went away. And when the wheat sprang up, the weeds appeared as well.

The servants said to the householder, "Sir, did you not sow good seeds in your field? Why is it that it has weeds?"

He said to them, "An enemy has done this."

Then the servants said, "Lord, permit us to go and gather up these weeds!"

But the Lord said, "No! Lest, in rooting up the weeds, you root up the wheat as well.

"Let both grow together until the harvest."

—Matthew 13:24–30

B. And Jesus spoke this parable about patience:

A man planted a fig tree in his vineyard, and he came seeking fruit from it and found none.

Then he said to the vine-dresser, "Behold, for three years now I have come seeking fruit on this fig tree, and I found none. Cut it down, therefore. Why does it still clutter up the ground?"

The vine-dresser replied, "Sir, let it alone one more year, while I dig around and manure it. Perhaps it may bear fruit. If it does not bear fruit in a year, then we will cut it down."

—Luke 13:4–9

Reflection

In two beautiful parables, Jesus lines up the dynamics of God's gentleness with us. In the weeds and wheat parable, God is portrayed as patient with the "weedy" aspect of our behavior. In the parable of the cared-for fig tree, Jesus relies on God's patience so that wayward humans are given more time to straighten out.

Look at the wheat field of Matthew's gospel. God is the farmer. His plan was that all creatures would turn out to be 100% good stuff—lions doing their lion-ey things; zebras doing their zebra-ey things; mollusks molluscating; vertebrates vertebrating…and so on. Best of all, humans were created to do their human-ey things—to live freely, act justly, love unselfishly, and worship God with thanks.

That was the plan. But "an enemy came and sowed weeds among the wheat and went away." So both the bad and the good grew up together, characterizing the human scene as a mix of both.

Christ's analysis of his time—that noble and ignoble traits existed side by side—is his analysis of our own time, also. It is the "state of the union message" for every nation of the world. It is the scuttlebutt at work, the gossip among friends and family, an accurate diagnosis of the Beauty and the Beast within us all. We are Jekyll and Hyde—70% and 30%—most good and partly bad, wheat and weeds, growing up together.

Does God get angry at such evidence of imperfection? Unlike the servants in the parable, God is the patient one; he does not destroy the wheat field because it appears to have a somewhat weedy aspect. It is the farmhands (it is *we*, not God) who manifest outrage at what is wrong with our world. The servants are the ones who sputter, "Lord, didn't you sow good seed in the field?" "Yes, I did." "Then why are weeds sprouting up all over? Can't you do things right?"

We can sputter like those servants. And we have. We complain against our own imperfections. "I wanted myself to be number one, in every way. And make lots of money, too! But I find it is not so. I am faulty at times. I can't remember things the way I used to. Many opportunities passed me by. I get tired quicker than I want to. I disappointed other people. And I've fallen short of the ideals I once had. Sometimes I have broken down—spiritually, mentally, financially, emotionally, physically. What's wrong, Lord? What's wrong with me?

"And what's wrong with some of the members of my family (especially _____!)? And why does the place where I work abound with imperfect people? And why are drivers on the road so inconsiderate? And what about bureaucrats, bankers, clerks, and doctors who keep me waiting? And what about everybody else who gets my goat? Why can't the world function just the way I'd like it to?!"

This is the way the farmhands grumbled to their master in Christ's parable. And this is the way we grumble against God.

The Master responds to all such tirades quite simply, and with amazing gentleness. "An enemy has done this," God says. But this soft answer does not turn away wrath, for the farmhands' immediate response is a blanket request for the annihilation of all annoyances: "Give us permission, Lord, to pull out all the weeds. Let me knock the living daylights out of all the flaws I find in my world, my church, my job, my family, and my friends. And, while I'm at it, let me also obliterate what I can't stand in everybody else I happen to meet. And make sure I have enough left to tear myself up, also...because I can't stand imperfections!"

But the Lord says *no*! That's it. God just tells us, without qualifications, not to do it. He does not utter wishy-washy declarations like, "Well, if you feel you *have to* weed out of your life what you feel to be offensive, okay...but be careful." God does not say that. He says "*No!*" And then he says, "Let both the good and the bad grow together. Do not judge yourself or others. Whenever you play the judge (and then the executioner) you destroy too much of the 70% good stuff in your world. No, *I'll* be the judge of what are weeds and what are wheat. That will come at the end of time. Leave judgment up to me. Your job is to make sure all things *grow*!"

What a beautiful message. But how do we fulfill this directive? We follow the lead of Christ's gentle example, as we see it in the second parable. Jesus tells us to think of a vineyard. In the middle of the vineyard is a somewhat troublesome fig tree. It's not doing very well. God is a "frustrated farmer," complaining about the lack of figs. He had planted it, cultivated it, then waited for results. Nothing. Zero productivity. So he decides to cut it down.

But the son intervenes, appealing for patience. "Wait, Father," he pleads. "Give your fig tree one more chance, a little more time. I will care for it with even more tenderness. I will teach all people—especially the wayward, unproductive people, like the fig tree. And I will nurture them until I wear myself out with fatigue. I will even die on the cross for them. Once they understand how large is the love we have for them, they will surely turn into worthwhile children of God!"

That is what Jesus said, on the day of parables, in Galilee. And that is what he did, on the hill of Golgotha, on Good Friday.

Prayer Setting

Think of two or three of your best friends. Remember how you first met. Then recall some of the "highlights" of your long associations, those experiences that gave you joy, delight, wisdom, encouragement...the realization that life was good. These could be likened to the "wheat" in Christ's parable—good times and good memories. No doubt, you and your friends hoped there would be nothing but good memories in the field of your friendships.

But there were less-than-happy experiences, also—the "lowlights." There was some misunderstanding, some thoughtlessness on both sides. There were a few occasions when one of you felt "used" or left out by the other. Things like that. These would be the "weeds" of your relationship.

Remember, though, that some of your "downers" turned out to be the cement for deeper, more trusting friendships. Sometimes, absence does make the heart grow fonder. When you were estranged from each other, you realized who it was you lost and how much it meant to you. Sometimes the "weeds" turned out to be "wheat."

So consider the whole of your friendships—their pluses and minuses. Let these considerations be your prayer today. And let it be not so much an "out-loud" prayer, but an "in-felt" prayer. You are feeling it; but let Jesus do the talking...

Jesus Talks to You

The memories of your friendships are very much like my parable of the wheat field, containing weeds as well as wheat. You can see, looking at your life, why my Father told his farmhands not to pull up the bad growth, lest the good get torn up with the worthless.

From one year to the next, you can't always tell how bad moods, or hurtful situations, will provide unforeseen learning experiences. Maybe you went through misery for a while. That was bad in itself. But it was good, also, in the sense that it taught you compassion for others. Remember how St. Peter sinned on Good Friday morning? And how bad he felt about it? That was not a noble thing he did; even so, by the way he endured his suffering, he grew to become much more understanding of the weaknesses of others, much less arrogant and judgmental. His first epistle shows how wonderfully he learned patience and compassion.

It's the same with you. The same with everybody. So, whether we talk about wheat fields or friendships, people in parishes or citizens of nations, fellow workers on the job or a family in the same house— you can see why my Father tells you to *cool it!*

You are not permitted to destroy yourself or the people in your world because of anything you consider an annoyance or a frustration. Your job is to make sure things grow.

You Pray to Jesus

Jesus, my Lord, you know my fears and my failures. I have been obnoxious at times. And I have flaws in my memory, quirks in my personality, wrongdoings and bad choices I'm ashamed of. You know this.

And you also know how mad I get because of the mistakes and irresponsible behavior of others. They make me so angry sometimes, I could scream. I'd like to have a magic weed killer that would take away all their faults and make them easier to get along with. Then I'd like to zap some of the people I go to church with, and rub shoulders with when I shop, and who drive in front of me on the highways, and who disagree with my politics.

Then, after getting rid of other people's faults, I want to turn my indignation on myself.

You know all this, my Lord. But I have done enough complaining about what's wrong with my world, with the people in my world, and with me. I don't want to act like those farmhands in your parable who wanted to destroy the wheat field because they were fed up with its weediness.

Enough of this griping and moaning and pointing out imperfections. Let me hear that *"No!"* coming from God your father. Let me learn not to destroy, but to make sure all things grow.

Also, my Lord, let me linger with the comforting words you gave me in the parable about the fig tree. You pleaded with God your father to give us time to grow. I'm so happy that you promised to jump-start me with nourishment whenever I get sluggish. It's good to be able to count on you.

But make sure I do more than just allow you to nourish me. Help me to be patient with others the same way. Get me to gentle down, my Lord. Help me to learn endurance and wait for growth to happen in this less-than-perfect world. Even with all the weeds, I'm glad I'm still alive.

If you stay close to me, Jesus, I know I will bear fruit—helped by your father's patience with me...and my patience with everybody else. Amen.

Chapter 13

Focusing on Found, Not Lost

(Luke 15–God Is Like a Woman Who Rejoices)

Jesus spoke this parable:
What woman, having ten drachmas, if she loses one, does not light a lamp and sweep the house and search carefully until she finds it? And when she has found it, she calls together her friends and neighbors and says, "Rejoice with me, for I have found what I had lost." Even so…there will be joy among the angels of God over one sinner who repents.   —*Luke 15:8–10*

Jesus spoke this parable to those who loved money:
The land of a certain rich man brought forth abundant crops, and he began to take thought within himself, saying, "I will pull down my barns and build larger ones, and there I will store up all my grain and my goods; and I will say to my soul, 'Soul, you have many good things laid up to last many years. Take your ease, eat, drink and be merry.'" But God said to him, "You fool! This very night, your life is demanded of you. Therefore, all those things you have acquired—whose will they be?"
                                                 —*Luke 12:13–21*

Reflection

Most of us, most of the time, don't identify with that scheming "grain commodities broker" in Christ's parable. He built extra barns so that he could live securely with what he hoarded. His wealth gave him no joy. It gave him only the assurance that he could "live it up" if he wanted to. But the only thing that energized him was the fervor of his protectiveness.

In contrast, the woman who finally located her lost coin is an endearing person we often can identify with. Because we've done the same ourselves, it is very easy to imagine how someone could be so "brimming over with joy" that she had to share her good fortune with everybody.

The lost coin in the story was a drachma. Its value was the equivalent of a full day's wages. In any country as poor as Galilee, it was precious. Even so, it seems that the woman spent more than what she found in order to splurge with her neighbors about the good fortune.

Practically speaking, it doesn't make sense to spend seven drachmas in order to celebrate the finding of one. But joy does crazy things sometimes. Haven't you "spent a bundle" just because things seemed to be looking up again—you got that lucky break that seemed to hint of more good fortune in the future? So you said yippee and broke out the champagne.

Even this superficial understanding of the parable shows that heaven promises to be a lot of fun. But the story has a deeper meaning, too. This parable comes in the middle of two others, in the famous "Triple Delight Stories About God" (Luke 15):

The Parable of the Found Sheep
The Parable of the Found Coin
The Parable of the Joyful Father Who Got Back His Prodigal Son.

Because of its context with the other two stories, the coin is probably something of much more value than pocket change. Probably it was one of the ten coins which were the "Sign of Covenant" between husband and wife. It was their traditional version of the wedding ring. In our Lord's time, it was an essential symbol of the social contract.

If this is the point of the story, it joins the other two parables to present us with a marvelously upbeat portrait of God. Jesus tells us three separate versions of how God is kind, compassionate, and rich in mercy. This is always so, especially whenever part of his covenant was lost and then found. God displays his brimming-over happiness the way a shepherd rejoices when he has found his sheep, the way a father rejoices when his errant son comes home, the way a woman rejoices when she has found her wedding ring.

Prayer Setting

First meditation: Identify with the housewife in Jesus' parable. Instead of pretending to take hours searching for a valuable coin, imagine that you are sitting beside your telephone, waiting for it to ring. Think back to an occasion when a good friend drifted away from you. (Don't think about whose fault it was, or who should have made the first steps to be reconciled. Just remember the pain of loss, because he or she was gone.)

Then imagine the telephone ringing and recall, once again, the joy you felt because friendship had returned. (Spend as much time with as many "reunited friendships" as you can remember. Let a spontaneous prayer of gratitude conclude this part of your meditation.)

Second Meditation: Think of some times when you have experienced loneliness from God. It can feel the same as being estranged from a friend. This separation came because of your own sins. Because of them, you, like the prodigal son, decided you weren't worthy to be in God's presence. Or maybe the sense of separation could have been caused by your being angry at God. You were hurt by the death, or great suffering, of a dear one; so you judged that God had treated you shabbily. Or you just drifted away from God—God and you seemed to have no shared interest.

Whatever the cause, there was something missing in your life. Somehow, you vaguely wished things could get straightened out, healed on the inside. You wanted more contentment in your life. You hoped to be found again. You hoped that "God would remember your phone number and call you."

And then it happened, somehow. Remember those times when light did come after the darkness—when the void was filled, when your heavy heart had bounce to it again, the phone did ring and you were there to answer it...

Jesus Talks to You

Hello? Is that you? I'm so glad you're still there. Let's talk a little...

Remember when you lost your friend, then found your friend again? Remember how the rift was healed and the quarrel finally settled? I was with you all the time. I arranged the circumstances so that it was easier for you to make up. I spaced the right amount of time so that the torn ligaments of hurt feelings could be healed. I rejoiced with you when the new love and friendship proved to be more patient and profound than it was before.

I'm so glad you did not become possessive in your relationship. That was the reason why your arguments began. You were possessive of your own opinions, your own time, your ideas of how things should be done. And your friend was caught up in a different set of fixed ideas. Then came bickering and maybe jealousy. Then came more inconsiderateness. Then, bam...you each went your separate ways.

Now you have learned not to be so possessive. You now know that it is disaster to be like that grumpy-greedy man in my second parable. He thought only of himself—his own security, his own barns, his own plans for living out the future.

Good for you that you never stayed with that life-style. I praise you for becoming more thoughtful than that. Many people have been helped because you learned how to be flexible in the demands of friendship. You worked at being a good listener, a sharer of joys, a giver and receiver of love that is genuinely unpossessive.

Keep up the good work. Let your 70% good side have more and more opportunities to grow.

And that goes for your relationship with my Father, too. If you could understand how much joy you give God when you return to him and let him love you, if you could sense even a smidgen of his expansive love for you, you would never run away again. You would never quit on life. Never.

You Pray to Jesus

Jesus, my Lord, thank you for telling me how much your Father loves me. I knew he did; but I forget, sometimes. I need your parables to remind me how much he wants to celebrate our friendship.

And speaking of friendship, thank you for all you've done "behind the scenes" to help in restoring my friendships. The spirit of your love has improved the quality and nobility of the love I have for all those I am honored to call friend.

Also, thank you, Jesus, for being that "housewife" in your parable. There have been times in my life when that was what you were. You spent many long days searching for me, pleading with me to come back. I don't know how you did it, exactly, but you did find an opening in my embittered heart and you helped me overcome those tendencies to get depressed. You did all this for me; and now I thank God that I let you love me—I let you love me your way.

I ask you a favor, Jesus. Help me be a vehicle of your joy for those who have become lost to others and even to themselves. Let me care about them and radiate goodness the way you do. Let me live with an ability to enjoy life, the way you showed me.

I never want to turn into that cross-grained miser in your other parable. I want to be like the woman who rediscovered what was lost. Like her, I want to claim my covenant with God and rejoice with all those friends who have made my life worthwhile. Amen.

Chapter 14

Mastering Patience

(Matthew 13–Jesus Unplugs Our "Quick Fuses")

[Now as the disciples were listening...Jesus went on to speak a parable, because he was drawing near to Jerusalem, and because they thought the Kingdom of God would appear immediately.] A man was going abroad and he called his servants and handed over his goods to them...Then, after a long time, the master returned and settled accounts...　　　　*—Matthew 25:14–30*

Reflection

Jesus had already "set his face toward Jerusalem." He knew he would be lifted up on the cross and then begin the gradual process of drawing all people to himself.

That was his idea about how developments would shape up. The apostles, however, begged to differ. And begged and begged and begged. They thought Christ's plan was foolhardy and slipshod. It left too much to chance; it was much too slow.

They wanted the Kingdom to appear immediately! According to their projections, the "Kingdom" was to be their version of heaven-on-earth—no unrest, no sadness or sickness, no troubles or taxes. The world would be blessed with peace and prosperity...and they would be on top of it all. Jesus and the apostles. The king and his cabinet.

They wanted all this, and they wanted it now! Jesus tried and tried to check their impetuosity. He insisted that his Kingdom would have results that would emerge so slowly they would not be very noteworthy.

Obviously, Jesus and his trainees thought of the future differently. So it's no wonder that our Lord told most of his parables urging his followers to develop the humble virtue of patience. This is the virtue that allows all the other virtues to grow. Above all, we must learn patience...patience...patience.

In story after story, the refrain comes through:

1. Don't get impatient with God—"The Parable of the Weeds and the Wheat" (Matthew 13—see chapter 12).

2. Don't get impatient with others—"The Parable of the Restless Servant":

> Jesus spoke this parable:
> Blessed is that servant whom the master, when he returns, shall find giving to the household their ration of food on time. But if that servant says to himself, "My master delays his coming," and begins to beat up on the menservants and the maidservants and begins to eat and drink and get drunk, the master of that servant will come on a day he does not expect, and in an hour he does not know, and will cut him asunder and make him share in the lot of the unfaithful.   —*Luke 12:42–46*

3. Don't get impatient with life—"The Parable of the Foolish Bridesmaids":

> Jesus spoke this parable:
> The kingdom of God is like ten bridesmaids who took their lamps and went forth to meet the bridegroom. Five of them were foolish, five were wise. The foolish ones took no oil with them...Then because the bridegroom was long in coming, they all became drowsy and slept. At midnight, a cry arose, "The bridegroom is coming, go forth to meet him!" The five who were ready went into the marriage feast...Then came the foolish ones who said, "Sir, open the door for us!" But he said, "I solemnly assure you, I do not know you."   —*Matthew 25:1–13*

The way to understand this parable is to identify with all ten maids of honor. Sometimes we act like those five wise bridesmaids. We have often remained composed, despite the lack of results. At other times, we are like the foolish ones, standing by the roadside and getting all upset because "the groom and his buddies kept their bachelor party going too long!" Doubtless, that was what happened. As a result, the parade to the bride's house didn't get started until very late (such goings-on really did take place in Christ's time)…and five frustrated bridesmaids could not endure such tardiness. So they quit.

Is Jesus correct in his estimate that we are patient only 50% of the time when delays upset our plans? Does that mean we are impatient half the time—honking our horns at anybody who holds us up and prevents us from immediately reaching our objectives?

Maybe it's not exactly 50% of the time. Maybe we are kind more than we are unkind toward other people's flaws. Perhaps we are better than blusterers when God delays things in his dealings with us. Let us presume that we most frequently take after the five wise and resilient maids of honor. We *do* realize that good results often take a long time to develop. We *can* prepare ourselves with a steadfast spirit. If we have to, we *are* able to "go with the flow." Most of the time.

Even so, we are both wise and foolish when we have to wait out those delays. We are long-suffering and we are short-fused. So Jesus keeps urging us to keep working on patience…and then work on it some more.

Prayer Setting

Imagine you are the parents of three very feisty, restless, antsy children. You have been driving four hours already, non-stop, to reach grandmother's house in time for supper. The children in the back seat are driving you crazy. "Aren't we there yet?" they keep asking. "Mommy, I'm bored!" "Daddy, my sister/brother hit me!" On and on and on. You get very upset. Their whining and fussing and "wanting things immediately" is not helping you get there. Not at all!

You can appreciate how you would feel, if you were a parent in

that situation. So you can understand how God feels about *your* bickering and complaining when your world does not turn the way you want it to: when good things don't show up, and bad things don't go away, as quickly as you would like.

Stay with this meditation as long as it seems good for you. Then balance your prayer. In your imagination, tap some memories of the times you faced trials with self-control. Remember when you have been patient with people and projects. (The best examples are memories from your job and your hobbies.)

1. Remember how glad you were that day when you did *not* tell off your boss, even though you were very upset. Also think of the times your coworkers were all losing their cool, but you stayed calm and collected.

2. Recall how much patience you have with your car, or computer, or other machine. Even though trouble came up, you still plodded along until things ran smoothly again. And recall how gentle you were with that apprentice on the job who was so clumsy and so slow to learn.

3. Consider your patience with the vegetables you grow or the flowers you help along in your garden. (If only you could treat people as gently as you do cucumbers!)

4. If you are a musician, or in the theater, or an athlete or coach, think of the endurance you've exercised in order to become a professional. Consider the discipline you had to learn before the skills became second nature to you.

5. If you are a good shopper, consider the lengths you'd go to for the special item and the price you are looking for.

6. Finally, if you are a parent, consider your steady encouragement as you urged your baby to eat, to talk, and take those first steps.

Recall to mind any or all of these gracious ways you proved yourself to be a person of steadfast endurance and indomitable patience. You took what was given you; then you worked and waited for results. Like the five wise women waiting for the bridal party to show up— and unlike the apostles who wanted the Kingdom to appear immediately—you showed a willingness to delay satisfaction. And you are blessed for it...

Jesus Talks to You

In many of my parables I have pleaded with you to develop patience. And now I see that you have more stories of your own to help you see the importance of not getting nervous about results. You've prayed over your Parable of the Antsy Children. And you've meditated on your own good memories suggested in that list of six categories.

Now is the time to make some resolutions. Put patience over your tendency to get fretful. When you are frustrated about my Father's slowness to answer your prayer, consider the boundaries within which God forces himself to operate. He seldom rearranges the laws of nature. Rarely will he allow miracles to pop up. And he never tampers with the free will of any human. So some things take a long time to get done because humans often drag their feet, and God will not use force to prod them on.

Sure, you get upset sometimes, when hopes crumble, or clumsiness cripples a project, or prayers don't get answered. I won't blame you for feeling bad. But I will blame you if your frustrations stop all progress, if setbacks cause you to quit on the future's possibilities.

I want you to be patient with divine tardiness and human dullness. Be as easy with friends and family as you are toward strangers who ask you directions. Be as patient with people as you are with tomatoes that need water, or your car that needs an oil change.

If you get angry at yourself because you failed to measure up to your ideals, heal those feelings by recalling the successes you've had in overcoming so many obstacles in the past. I like the way you keep going, despite delays. I want you to know how proud I am of you.

This kind of upbeat meditation will help you identify with the five wise bridesmaids. Your good memories will "keep the lamps burning"; and these reflections can be a soothing presence for the times you want to scream out "What's wrong!" because your world...or your family...or yourself...frustrates you.

Patience is still the bottom line, my disciple, my friend. Your work is not to fall asleep on life, like the fools who cannot handle delays. Your work is to accept what is, with the time that you have, and make "what is" a little better than it was.

You Pray to Jesus

Jesus, my Lord, let me always remember the good things that have developed in my life. Yes, I have nurtured plants and flowers and vegetables. I have been gentle with children. I even admit nursing my car with great care, every time it goes bonkers. I have also made shy people feel at home, and have slowly gone through the paces for those who were learning a new job.

Thanks to your help, I've bounced back from the downers that have come my way. I thought the world was collapsing, but it wasn't. At times, I thought I could never love again, but I did. There were times when I decided that the parade had passed me by, but it hadn't. And from all these good experiences, I know I'll have your strength to keep me going, until I make it all the way to heaven.

Help me to feed patience with courage, and to nourish endurance with good cheer. And let me never forget your promises. They will not often come immediately; but they are worth waiting for... Amen.

Chapter 15

Letting Go of Grudges
(Matthew 18–Gratitude Heals Bad Moods)

Jesus spoke this parable:
A king desired to settle accounts with his servants....One was
brought in who owed him ten thousand talents...[approximate-
ly $450 million!] The servant fell down and pleaded with his
king: "Have patience with me and I will repay you." Moved with
compassion, the master of that servant released him and forgave
him the debt. But as that servant went out, he met one of his fellow servants who owed him one hundred denarii [about $75!].
The man laid on his fellow servant and throttled him, saying,
"Pay what you owe me!" His fellow servant fell down and began
to plead with him, "Have patience with me and I will pay you
all." But he would not! He went away and cast his fellow servant
into prison...His master called the man and said to him, "You
wicked servant! I forgave all your debt...Should you not have
had compassion on your fellow servant, as I had compassion on
you?" And his master, being angry, handed him over to the tor-
turers...So also my Father will do to you, if you do not forgive
one another from your hearts.

—Matthew 18:23–35

Reflection
The contrast in this parable is the sweet, then bitter, mood of the main
character. We see two debts that have two different stories to tell.
They help us realize there is a bit of the villain in us all. Even though
Jesus plays him up in such a larger-than-life fashion, the man's quick
mood swings and severe demands for swift justice hold up a mirror to
the worst part of our 30% bad side.

The man must have been a powerful politician. Most likely, he was a governor of one section of the Roman Empire, or a Procurator like Pontius Pilate. He would have managed a rather lucrative area of the world, answerable only to Caesar Augustus. As Jesus tells the story, the man owed ten thousand talents to the empire. Roughly, that amount of money would be about $450 million today, give or take a few thousand. Most modern translators would have us read that the individual owed his master a "huge amount." But, to a beggar or a child, a $20 bill is a huge amount. Jesus—master storyteller that he is—specifies those facts which are so important to the contrast in the parable. All listeners can draw their own conclusion about how huge the debt was.

Jesus then takes you to Rome's version of Washington, D.C. A department similar to our Internal Revenue Service has gathered facts and delivered its report to Caesar. Put yourself in the man's place. Feel his agony. He has been reported. He is disgraced. The only prospect is either the death penalty or hard labor someplace. He falls on his knees and blurts out the first dumb thing that comes into his head: "Master, be patient with me, and I will pay back all the graft I took!"

"Who are you kidding?" most Caesars would have said. "You have no bank accounts left. No contacts. No chance for any new connections, now that you are in disgrace. You couldn't earn even $200 a year. How could you pay back $450 million?"

That should have been the end of the story. But it wasn't. The end, as Jesus tells it, is what movie critics of today would call contrived. They would give the scene thumbs down. Caesar said to the chiseler pleading for his life these most amazing words: "Okay, I forgive you. Your debt is wiped clean. You don't owe anybody anything. Do better next time!"

Wow! What a tremendous turnabout. This lavish gift of mercy is almost as lavish as the Son of God becoming flesh of Mary and growing up and getting crucified to save us from death and forgive us our sins. And then he opened heaven for us where we will live forever with joy beyond our fondest hopes.

Of course, the man in the parable is elated. He is relieved. Energized. Already he starts to plan how he will return to his post, proving trustworthy from now on. He wants to make sure Caesar's hunch about him was right.

Imagine yourself in his place, as he returns home and tells his friends about his good fortune. Naturally, he puts the facts in the best light possible—how lucky he was, how kind his "good old buddy Caesar" was, how (as they were having a couple of drinks afterward) the Emperor told him that other servants might be inveterate swindlers, but not him... He was worthy of another chance!

A lovely scene...for a while. The mood was euphoric, the focus was gratitude, the air was charged with talk of fresh starts. But none of this lasted very long. The ex-swindler came upon a man who was in his debt. (It was for one hundred denarii—about $75!) He collared his debtor and demanded: "Pay me what you owe me! If I don't get the cash right now, I'm taking you to the courthouse and you'll be thrown in jail! And I mean *now*!"

The contrast between the debt forgiven and the debt demanded is 1 to 600,000! The character who was forgiven by Caesar had surely been given more mercy and patience than he is now asked to give to a fellow servant.

(Note the genius of Jesus as a storyteller. The man who owed $75 falls on his knees and pleads his case in the same way, and with the same words, as the swindler did when he was before Caesar.)

The man who was forgiven had already gotten used to the day-in, day-out routine of things back home. The magnificent good fortune of a few weeks back was now buried in the dormant side of his memory. He promptly forgot the earlier mercy bestowed on him. He had work to do, requisitions to honor, logistics to determine, justice to abide by. Now, there was this matter of the $75 *he* was owed. "Pay up!"

Prayer Setting

Imagine that you have a large storeroom of home movies containing films of your best days, top experiences, those wonderful occasions when good fortune came your way. The room contains, among other things:

Spiritual Blessings: Included here would be your good instincts toward God, a genuine spirit of prayer, the ability to be quiet with your thoughts, the capacity to be grateful for what you have received, the inspirations that sometimes come unbidden...such things as these.

Physical and Material Blessings: Included here would be a good brain, a body able to perform thousands of human functions, a capacity to enjoy your comforts...and so many more items of God's creative beneficence so often taken for granted.

Filial and Social Blessings: Included here would be the members of your family who have stayed loyal to you; also, all those people who have befriended you along the way, some of them good friends still.

And, of course, *Christ's Death and Resurrection:* Because of *his* gift, you live with the certain hope of heaven. That $450 million is nothing when compared to this gift. Money cannot go further than the grace; but Jesus has given you a gift that will last forever!

These are some of the good things that have been filmed and stored in your personal library. Remember how you take out a film or two, every now and then. Maybe on Thanksgiving you are grateful to your family. Maybe during Holy Week, you thank Jesus for his love. But normally, these films are given no attention. They are just dumped into the closet of possessed forgetfulness.

Next, in your imagination, walk resolutely (and self-righteously) up to the houses of those people who owe you money, or who should be kinder to you than they are. These individuals merge into the living room of one house. Joining them are your real enemies—those who have mistreated you in any way.

There they are! You enter the house and prepare to tell them all off...or to get revenge...or to show, by your silence, how you scorn them! You are just on the verge of displaying some form of retaliation when you see Jesus in the background. Your heart turns over for a moment. You wonder, "What is Jesus doing with people I dislike? I naturally presumed that Jesus would judge everybody the very same way I do!"

You regain composure and show respect for the Lord. Jesus moves slowly to the center of the room. Your antagonists are on one side. You are on the other. The seminar begins...

Jesus Talks to You

I want to balance the good and the bad side of your life, my friend. I want you to see both the marvelous gifts of mercy and good fortune done to you and for you. Along with these considerations, take a good look (a fair look) at the injustices you have experienced and the unkind treatment that has come your way.

Please look at the videos of the good material, first. As you do, you will be amazed at your good luck. Try to recall how you actually felt as these wonderful experiences happened to you. Then remember what happened a short time *after* they took place...as you got used to them and quickly drifted back into boredom, taking for granted the marvels that fell in your lap.

When you've finished viewing the film clips about yourself, begin to meditate on the love and mercy I showed you when I died on the cross for you. I want you to really understand how much I care about you, and that I suffered my passion so that you could be given perfect happiness.

Finally, turn off the VCR. Pray in silence for a while, then join me in the kitchen. The people you don't like will still be with me. We will share a meal together. In our company, I want you to pray out loud for the virtue of forgiveness. Ask me to help you forgive those who have done you wrong. As you have received mercy from me, I want you to give mercy to others. I want you to live with forgiveness—to get it right and give it right.

You Pray to Jesus

My Lord, I know that I have to work harder developing my 70% good side, and to fight stronger against the meanness in me. I am so tempted to think only of getting back at people who have mistreated me or let me down. Like that wicked servant in your parable, I sometimes forget all the love I got from you, and all the good that has come from so many people, in so many ways. Too often I have let these marvels of my life fade out of sight.

Jesus, let me take those videos of "Good Things That Happened to Me" and bring them back home again. Help me to be more attentive to all my "Givens" and to do better with your command to love in the way you taught me to.

Maybe I still can't completely forgive those who have hurt me. But with your help I will do a better job than I have been doing.

Little by little, I will be able to dedicate myself to thankfulness. I will live like that servant who was revived and felt such a burst of exuberant gratitude, because his debt to Caesar was suddenly wiped clean. And the fear of dying will never more torment me. You have given me a hope that will live forever, fresh dignity because I know you love me, and the very best of reasons for relenting my hard lines and allowing your mercy to be my way of mercy given to others. Amen.

Chapter 16

Including Other People

(Luke 15–Jesus Loves the Prodigal and his Brother)

Jesus said…

The prodigal son went off to a distant land, where he squandered his money on loose living. Coming to his senses at last, he said within himself, "I will return to my father and say, 'Father, I have sinned against God and against you. I am no longer worthy to be called your son. Treat me as one of your slaves!'" With that, he set off to his father's house. While he was still a long way off, his father caught sight of him and was deeply moved with compassion. He ran out to meet him, threw his arms around his neck and kissed him. The son said, "Father, I have sinned against God and against you. I am no longer worthy to be called your son." The father cut off the son's speech! Then he said to the servants: "Quick! Bring out the finest robe and put it on him…Let us eat and celebrate, because my son was dead and has come back to life!" And the celebration began.

Meanwhile the elder son was still in the field, working. As he came near to the house, he heard music and dancing. Calling one of the servants, he inquired what this meant. The servant said, "Your brother has come home. And your father has made a celebration because he has got him back safe." The older brother was angered and would not go in. So his father came out to him and begged him to. But he answered, "Behold, all these many years I have been serving you and have never disobeyed you. And you never gave me a celebration so that I might have a party with my friends…!" Then the father said, "Son, you are always with me. All that is mine is yours. But we must rejoice, for your brother was dead and has come to life again; he was lost and now is found." —*Luke 15:11–32*

Reflection

Many books and countless sermons have already mined the treasure of God's mercy told in this parable. The attention paid to the prodigal son continues to assure the world that God's expansive mercy is offered to all, no matter how wasted the life.

But, for the purposes of this book, it would be better to give prominence to the *elder* brother, that stay-at-home, hardworking individual who (at least on one occasion) let envy and bitterness get the better of him.

Indeed, it seems to be Jesus' purpose that we should give more notice to this man than to his kid brother. St. Luke's gospel sets up all three parables in Chapter 15 as a response to the Pharisees who criticized Jesus for being too friendly toward those who were considered unacceptable by the "good people" of society.

To really understand the thrust of Christ's intentions, we need to reflect on the storyline: Tax collectors and sinners were all gathering around to hear Jesus, at which the Pharisees and the scribes murmured, "This man welcomes sinners and eats with them" (Luke 15:1–2).

That is the setting. The animosity behind their "murmuring" was growing to fever pitch. These "law-abiding people" were bent on destroying Christ's work and dishonoring his person. They were even plotting to kill him.

Jesus, for his part, never stooped to their level of meanness. Instead of retaliating, he praised the very people who were out to get him. When the father in the parable was speaking to his older son, it was Jesus speaking to the Pharisees: "My friends, you have been dear to God for many years, many centuries. The Father really appreciates you for all the energy you have in the doing of good works and all the exemplary behavior you display and the honest piety and awesome courage you have, as you treasure the laws that have been handed down for your good.

"God really appreciates it. But you must rejoice when other people experience the Father's love in a different way. Many of these people are not as careful of the law as you are. Some are pagans and do not know the law at all. Others were sinners for a time; but now they want to return to me. These people need mercy just as much as you need praise. They are the causes for God's joy when they straighten out and join the circle of my friends. So you must rejoice because God loves those you find it hard to love. And so do I. If you really love God you will, little by little, learn to love them, too."

That is what Jesus said to his severest critics. The father in the parable did not scold his older son. He did not "tell him off" for refusing to take part in the festivities. He didn't let him stew outdoors, leaving him all alone to "teach him a lesson." None of these things. The father went out to where his son was having that pity-party all by himself. He pleaded with the sullen sibling, begging him to come in and have a good time.

So the moral of the story is twofold: 1) The father loves his prodigal son for having the courage to repent and the wisdom to come back home. 2) He also praises the dutiful son for the good—the steady, dependable, productive good—by which he proved himself to be deserving of his father's gratitude.

Both children are beloved by God, each for different reasons. They both represent different sides of our personality. But while we can identify with the prodigal sometimes, we are the elder son *most* of the time. We must work very hard so that we don't fall into that 30% mean side of us which could so easily turn us into someone ruined by envious thoughts and sullen behavior.

Prayer Setting

Pretend you are in the crowd when Jesus tells his famous parable. Every time he wants to refer to you as "somebody like the prodigal son" he makes a sign that you shall stand alone, right in front of him. Then, as he refers to the similarities you have with the older son, he wants you to mingle with the crowd. You are in the habit of thinking like the brother who would not take part in the feast.

As the Lord speaks, he enunciates very slowly and deliberately, putting in many silences whenever he wants the words to really hit home. Pay serious attention to his words and his silences.

After speaking, he invites you to take a walk with him. Just the two of you. As you go, Jesus talks about some of the thoughts that are most dear to him...

Jesus Talks to You

Yes, my disciple, my friend, you sometimes behave like the little brother, sometimes like the big brother. Whenever you returned to God, like the prodigal, and asked for help to straighten your life out, you did well. You must know how pleased my Father is in you.

I also want you to know how good God feels when you have been like the older brother. It's easy to believe God's love when there's a climax in your life, when you were honest and humble enough to ask for mercy. It's not so easy to understand God's love when you are simply doing your duty in your day-to-day world. Because it seems that everybody else takes you for granted, it's a short step to believe that God does, too.

And then—in the mood of "nobody appreciates me!"—all those faults of the "obedient and dutiful son" make their appearance. You become victimized by your own good deeds; or you get downhearted when other people get the breaks, or have the money, or receive the applause that you missed out on. Do not compare yourself with the talents or the accomplishments or privileges of others. Don't think that you are nothing because you are not like somebody else. God my Father does not undervalue you just because he makes a big fuss over somebody else.

It's easy to warm up to any part if it was *you* who performed some heroic act and this is who the party is *for*. It is not so easy to feel good about somebody else's celebration when you feel you have been sidelined...and all you have to show for yourself are the ordinary humdrum tasks that you have done, and done so well, for such a long, long time.

Because it's tougher to be *un*dramatically good, you must work all the harder to keep up your spirits in those "blah" areas of your life. And you must cultivate an honest self-love for all the good you've done this way.

Notice what I said is an honest self-love. That means not comparing yourself to anybody else, not wishing you were different from who you are, not wanting to change positions or projects with whomever it is you are tempted to envy. You must learn to never mind how God is dealing with anybody else (or how *anybody* is dealing with anybody else). Stay with your own gifts, your own capacities. Consider your life as a positive accomplishment. And say to yourself, "Yes. My world is better off for my having been in it."

Then let God reply: My daughter, my son, I really do appreciate all the good things you have done in your life. You have been a plus. You have made me proud. Now come in out of the cold and take an active part in celebrating all the different ways my friends have made me glad that I created them.

You Pray to Jesus

My Lord, don't let me look at life as if it were a big bulletin board where I see only the accomplishments and awards honoring other people. If I keep being so sensitive about those things, I'll soon grow weary with what I'm doing and then I'll mope about and feel sorry for myself. Indeed, I'll end up missing out on a lot of happiness, just like that elder brother in your parable.

Help me really listen to the way your Father praised his older son. Let me be attentive when he says that he *is* pleased by my ordinary tasks, done well. He can't break out the champagne for every situation. I know that. His praise for me is generally a low-key recognition. But it is recognition. Let me never forget that part.

I want to keep working out of the 70% good side of me. Most of this work will be the unspectacular (and usually unregarded) doing-of-my-duty. Even so, it is my duty, my good use of gifts, my contribution to the plus of creation. And it will be my way of earning that good regard of God your Father as he warmly welcomes me into the celebration of never-ending joy, where I will discover that, after all is said and done, my drudgeries and duties were not so bad! They were worthwhile, and worthy of your Father's praise. Amen.

Chapter 17

Helping Jesus Do his Work

(Matthew 13–Christ Lightens Our Worry Load)

Jesus said:

The meaning of the parable is this: The seed is the word of God.

1. Those seeds that fell upon the hard path are they who hear the word of God but do not bother to understand it. Then the evil one comes and snatches away the seed from their heart.

2. Those seeds on the rock are they who, when they have heard, receive the word with joy. But they have no root. They believe for a while, but when trouble or persecution come, they fall away.

3. Those seeds that fell among the thorns are they who have heard the word of God but, as they go their way, they are choked by the cares and riches and the pleasures of life… (Luke 8:4–15)

…but the cares of the world and the deceitfulness of riches, and the desires about other things enter in and choke the word and it is made fruitless… (Mark 4:1–20)

…but the cares of this world and the seductive glamor of riches choke the word and it is made fruitless… (Matthew 13:1–23)

4. But the seed sown on the good ground are they who, with a right and good heart, hear the word of God, hold it fast and bring forth fruit in patience.

Reflection

Twenty centuries ago, in the backwater region of Galilee, Jesus and those who listened to him lived a simple life. There was farming, grazing flocks, craftsmen's trades, and not much more than that. Transportation was by foot, or donkey, or maybe horse or camel.

Agriculture was still at the primitive stage.

So when Jesus wanted to tell people that meriting the happiness of heaven demanded effort on their part (it was not "automatic," with God doing everything), he had to speak in a language that was familiar. He could not talk about the upkeep of automobiles or the complexity of cable TV. They weren't invented yet. He talked about a farmer sowing seed from his basket hoping it would land on good soil.

We don't farm that way any more. Old fashioned metaphors are understandable...but their "zip" is gone. Galilean customs are unfamiliar in today's world.

So let me take some literary license and rework the parable, telling it as Jesus might have done if he had lived today...

The God-Movement of Grace is like four cars that went into a gas station. One car was a mess. It had a slipped transmission, rusty pipes, cracked battery—a total nothing! When it got pushed into the gas station, it still refused to move...no matter how good the gas was.

The second car had many good parts. The only trouble was that the muffler was low-hung and the tires were bald. As long as the car traveled on smooth roads, fine. But as soon as it hit bumps and potholes on the side streets, forget it. It broke down, even though the gas was high octane!

The third car was good, clean, and cared for. However, it was overloaded with extra gear. This "just in case material" was lashed onto the roof. Because of it, the car could not drive through tunnels or drive over a span-bridge when the wind was high. Any breeze stiffer than 25 mph would poke its fingers into the stuff on the rooftop and toss everything into the sea.

The fourth car was a winner. The family had cared for it. They knew where they were going. They showed kindness and were thoughtful of each other as they went along. And this car got 30, 40, even 50 miles to the gallon!

In this paraphrase, Jesus is the gas station attendant. The Holy Spirit is the travel agent, giving us directions and the original momentum to reach our destination. Grace is the unleaded gasoline. It is all good grace, but we cannot simply rely on the gasoline to get us there. We must do something, too. We must keep the "vehicle" in good shape and not overburden ourselves with the cares of this world, the anxieties about finances, envy about other people, or the desire to control everyone and everything in our world.

It is only by streamlining such demands within us—and mastering our bad attitudes—that we will make it to our Christ-promised destiny.

Prayer Setting

Imagine different times of your life fitting each of those categories of cars. Perhaps, some time back, you ignored the love of God and disregarded his challenges to you. Worldly preoccupations completely filled you up. This would be like the seed that fell on the road where birds of the air devoured everything.

You realized that living in such a way sooner or later drained you dry—like a car with slipped transmission and rusty pipes. Worldly concerns were never designed to get you home. So much for category #1!

Next, imagine yourself in the second illustration. You might have felt quite close to God when you received your first holy communion. Maybe you thrilled to the gospel message on some other momentous occasions. And the religious side of Christmas and Easter used to be important to you. But then—like a car without shock absorbers, or like seed without roots that was scorched by the burning sun—you didn't want to continue in the faith as soon as troubles came. The pressure of the "group" making fun of you, or the trauma of some personal bad fortune, or the sudden death of a dear one, or some scandals in the church, or puzzlement about an article of faith—such difficulties may have caused a breakdown in your perseverance.

Or maybe there was nothing at all dramatic about your sundered relationship with God. Perhaps your situation fits into that third category—where weeds, growing with the good seed, were allowed to continue until they took over completely and strangled the good stuff—when your car was so overburdened it couldn't squeeze through the low overheads of the trip. Perhaps you didn't even notice how the cares of the world and anxieties about other things gradually became dominant in your life.

There is one car left. You've waxed it and gassed it up and given it the full check-up. This personifies the 70% good side of you. You are preparing to continue enjoying the trip as long as God sees fit to keep you alive. And you are equipped—having neither too much nor too little baggage—to make it all the way to your destiny.

The provider of this high octane energy is, of course, the Lord. He comes out of his office to give you some last-minute instructions...

Jesus Talks to You

Before you start on your journey, I want to balance warnings with encouragement, challenges with common sense.

When I keep telling you not to worry, and forewarn you against the danger of anxieties choking your life, I'm not telling you not to plan for the future. Indeed, I spent most of my time and energy training the disciples, with the future of the church in mind. And just before I died, I took out an "insurance policy" for my mother. When I told John to "behold your mother," I made sure she would be provided for.

Another thing. As I warn you not to get discouraged, I'm not suggesting that you turn into an unfeeling block of granite. After all, I was discouraged when the people of Jerusalem rejected me. I was so saddened that I wept. And Judas' betrayal hurt me deeply. But I was not controlled by these emotions. I refused to let dismay block my determination to continue.

So with you. When I tell you not to be anxious, I mean don't worry about those things you can't do anything about. And when I tell you not to be choked off by the desires for wealth or prominence, I do not imply that you should become a hermit or live in isolation. I mean don't let the 30% bad side of you take over your life.

In all this, you must plan well how much baggage (and how much emotional baggage) you should take along. You must become more flexible and more "lightweight"—letting go of a lot of excess concerns about securities and possessiveness.

I want you to come home: all the way home, to heaven's perfect happiness. You can do it...but you have to get into that fourth car. Make sure you remain as my good seed, flourishing in good soil, well-weeded, free from too many preoccupations that could drain your life away.

You Pray to Jesus

Jesus, my Lord, help me pack up for my trip through life with just the right things I need for my journey. Let me keep my concerns for the future; but make sure I discard the worries about situations I cannot change, and those headaches about the tomorrows that haven't come yet.

Let me be glad, my Lord, that I have a sensitive nature. I'm not going to hold back tears when I lose a friend or suffer the loss of a loved one. I will never pretend it doesn't bother me if I am rejected or if some of my most cherished ideas are scorned. Sure, these things hurt. After all, Lord, you felt bad for the same reasons. Just show me how not to let disappointments get the best of me. I want to keep going, so I must refuse to let either worries or hurt feelings bottle me up.

Instead of that, let me be grateful for my friends, healthy with a disposition that keeps hope alive, and glad that I have a good destiny to look forward to.

Well, that's enough talking, Lord. Time to finish the travel arrangements, check the maps once more, get rid of the extra baggage.

(At this time, pray silently for a while as you meditate on what parts of your life must go—the favorite anxieties, the hurt feelings you "cherish" within yourself, the negative opinions others have of you, the bad habits or compulsions you still cling to. Imagine yourself leaving all this behind. When you finish the meditation, conclude:)

I'll see you at the next gas station down the road, Jesus. Promise me you'll be there. I want to ask you to go with me, all the way. Amen.

Chapter 18

Noticing Needs and...

(John 6–Jesus Praises Andrew and the Barley Boy)

Now the Pharisees, who were fond of money, were listening to Jesus. And they began to sneer [at his teachings]. So he said to them, "There was a certain rich man who used to clothe himself in purple and fine linen and who feasted sumptuously every day. There was also a poor man, named Lazarus, who lay at his gate, covered with sores, and longing to eat the crumbs that fell from the rich man's table...And it came to pass that the poor man died and was borne away by the angels into Abraham's bosom. Then the rich man also died and was buried...The rich man pleaded with Abraham, "Send Lazarus to my father's house, for I have five brothers, and warn them not to come to this place of torment." Abraham said, "They have Moses and the prophets; let them listen to them." But he answered, "No, Father Abraham; but if someone from the dead goes to them, they will repent." Abraham replied, "If they do not listen to Moses and the prophets, they will not believe even if someone were to rise from the dead!" —Luke 16:14,19–31

The Passover was near. When Jesus lifted up his eyes [from prayer] and saw that a very great crowd had come to him, he said..."How shall we get bread so that all these people may eat?"...One of his disciples, Andrew, the brother of Simon Peter, said to him, "There is a young boy here who has five barley loaves and two fish..." Jesus said, "Make the people recline." Jesus then took the bread, gave thanks, and distributed them to those reclining; and likewise the fish, as much as they wished. They then gathered up what was left over, and they filled twelve baskets with the fragments of the five loaves left over by those who had eaten. When the people had seen the sign which Jesus had worked, they said, "This is indeed the Prophet who is to come into the world."   *—John 6:1–15*

Reflection

Strange and unfamiliar as the settings may be, these two stories speak about ordinary attitudes in reaction to ordinary situations. They show how well Jesus understands both our naughty side and our unnoticed heroism.

The word naughty is used in its original sense—as Jesus used it when he castigated the Pharisees who "brought to naught" God's purposes concerning themselves (Luke 7:30). Our Lord was talking about that "nothing doing" of the rich man who took care of himself, but did nothing for others. This unnamed individual was not wicked. There is no mention of him breaking any commandment or trashing the environment or abusing people. Why he was sent to hell was, literally, "for nothing." That is, he did "naught" about someone he should have done some good for. He didn't even notice the poor beggar beside his garbage can. He didn't even see him!

As the story continues, the rich man, now in hell, asks Moses to warn his brothers, "lest they also come to this place of torment." You see, the seven brothers are also afflicted with the "I-just-look-out-for-myself" syndrome. They were so busy with their own pleasures and preoccupations, they didn't have compassion for anybody.

Jesus puts into the mouth of Moses his own reply to the selfish brothers: "They have the Sacred Scriptures to warn them that they must think of others, not only of themselves." "No," said the rich man, "they'll never bother to pray over the Scriptures. But if somebody should come back from the dead, they'll perk up!"

"They will not!" said Jesus, in reply. "If they refuse to be moved by God's words in the Bible, they will not change their life-style even if somebody should die on a cross for them and then come back from the dead! Even after the magnificent events of Holy Week, they will not alter their determination to be self-absorbed consumers, devoted to their own pleasures and their own pursuits."

Sometimes we are "naughty," too. Just for argument, let's say we work out of that bad attitude 30% of the time. That would mean on 3 out of 10 occasions, we act like the thoughtless pleasure-seeker in St. Luke's gospel. But do not grieve too much for your naught-i-ness. You can't start seeing what you failed to do; that's because you failed to notice it in the first place. So how can you remember what you didn't see before? The best way to not grieve Jesus is to follow the example of St. Andrew the apostle and the boy with the barley loaves and fish.

Because he stays nameless in the gospels, we'll call him Barley Boy. St. Andrew and Barley Boy exemplify the two fundamental preconditions of compassion. Andrew was a "noticer"; the boy was a "cooperator."

Even though the multiplication of the loaves and fishes was an actual event, the gospels (St. John's gospel in particular) present it more as a parable than an episode. It is a masterful story of how we all should love.

It begins with our Lord's words: "I have compassion on the people. If I do not nourish them, they will faint on their journey." Then, after pointing out compassion to be the point of this "Eucharist" (and all Eucharists to follow), Jesus says to Philip, "There's a lot of mouths to feed, here in this desert. How are we going to work this out, Philip?" "Beats me!" was Philip's typical reply. But then Andrew came to the rescue. He noticed a boy pushing a small pushcart, obviously hoping to make a little profit selling a few fish sandwiches. Jesus called for the boy to come closer; then he asked him to contribute to the cause. The boy agreed. (This was the first recorded "church collection" taken up to feed the hungry.)

Andrew noticed what was going on. Barley Boy agreed to cooperate in a good cause. That's what love is all about. They both "brought to something" God's purposes of compassion. They were "some-ty"— they were not "naught-y."

Prayer Setting

Take yourself to the top of a hill, or beside a calm, clear lake. It is a lovely afternoon. You are alone, because you choose to be. Relax.

Soon you are joined by two people you admire. (They could be people still living, people from your past, or people from history. The only conditions are that they be good, and that you admire them.) They are thoughtful and gentle. You have always appreciated how they have shown such compassion toward others. They are aware of life and responsive to it. Imagine yourself greeting them in whatever way seems right.

After you settle down, praise them for their goodness. Tell them about some of the things you most admire in them. Don't work too hard at expressing yourself. Just let the words spill out. See how comfortable they are as they accept your compliments.

Then let the roles be reversed. Let them praise you for your kindness. Let them remind you about how sensitive you have been to the needs of others. Just like St. Andrew, you noticed people and were concerned for them. Allow your friends to compliment you for the "Andrew within you." And make sure you accept their praise as easily and as courteously as they accepted yours.

Let your friends also remind you how often you agreed to help where help was called for. You were asked to contribute time and/or money for a good cause. And you did. You were asked to drive a person to the airport, or visit someone in the nursing home, or listen to somebody's troubles...and you said okay. Like Barley Boy, you have been blessed by Jesus many times over for your works of love...

Jesus Talks to You

Yes, I'm here, too. And I want to share your quiet place for a few minutes.

My friend, I hope that you will often return to the memory of how you noticed needs, like Andrew, and how you responded to needs, like the boy with the bread and fish. The way to get better about this work of having compassion is to recall those times when you were at your best.

But please, please, please don't remember those good deeds in order to feel sorry for yourself. My heart grows sad when I see so many good people ruin their goodness by saying things like, "Yes, I did such-and-such a good work for so-and-so... And I spent my energy for this one... And I used up many of my free afternoons helping out that one... And see how they take me for granted. They never thanked me! They don't even think about returning the favor and helping me out once in a while! Boo hoo!"

See? They wreck their good hearts on the rocks of self-pity. Don't do that. Keep saying to yourself: "I did good because it was good to do!" Period! Then you will become more and more insightful—you will grow by leaps and bounds in your capacity to be sensitive to the needs of others.

I'm not going to scold you for your negligence in the past. I know all about those times. I felt bad when you acted like that rich man in my parable, and like his brothers. They were so filled up with their own concerns they didn't notice anybody else. When you loved like them, you "brought to naught" God's purposes of love. But the past is past. You cannot make it up.

The best way to not be naughty is to develop a better and broader compassion. I urge you to be more alert to the needs of others. Be especially sensitive to those needs—especially in your family—which are rarely put into words. They may seldom talk about their deepest feelings and dearest wants, but they are there. And blessed are you if you respond before they get up the courage to ask you.

In these situations, and many more besides, keep working on your 70% good side. St. Andrew and Barley Boy will be cheering you on. They will give you the pep talks. I will give you the pep. Count on it.

You Pray to Jesus

Jesus, my Lord, keep me working out of my good side. Let me put a watchful guard over my tendency to be preoccupied about my own concerns. I never intend to be thoughtless. Sometimes I just get immersed in what I am doing and in what I plan to do. Even so, I realize it doesn't matter whether I meant to be cruel, or I just didn't notice. The results of neglect are the very same: Lazarus is still starving outside, somewhere…

Never permit me, Lord, to weasel out of love with wimpy words like "I didn't see him begging!" "I forgot all about it!" Make sure I get as good at noticing those in need as St. Andrew was. And let me be a cheerful giver, too.

That rich man in your parable, Lord, never had a name. You called him by the vague title of "A certain rich man"—he was "blah." Our world is very impressed with the rich and famous. We consider them "somebodies" and always know their names. You judge people differently. You talked about that man-of-influence as a "nobody" because he "brought to naught" God's purposes.

But Lazarus did have a name. He was someone you loved and you saw to it that he got to heaven. Let me love him, as you did…and love all the "Lazaruses" in my life.

Then I will be called by my first name, too. No more will I be naughty…or nameless. I will be your "somebody," nourished by the food of you and the words of you. With your help, I'll not faint on my journey. I'll make it all the way home. Amen.

Chapter 19

Passing Our Final Exams

(Matthew 25–Luke 10, Christ the King Is a Good Professor)

A lawyer got up to test Jesus, saying, "Master, what must I do in order to gain eternal life?" The answer was: "You shall love the Lord your God with all your heart, soul, strength, and mind," and "You shall love your neighbor as yourself." But the lawyer, wishing to justify himself, said, "And who is my neighbor?" Jesus said: "A certain man was going from Jerusalem to Jericho, and he fell in with robbers who stripped him and beat him and went their way, leaving him half-dead. And it happened a certain priest...and likewise a Levite...passed him by...But a certain Samaritan, as he journeyed, came upon him, and seeing him, was moved with compassion. And he went up to him and bound up his wounds, pouring on oil and wine. And setting him on his own beast, he brought him to an inn and took care of him..."

—Luke 10:25–37

Reflection

Of all the themes that Jesus considered important, the one that was tops on his list was "How to Get Yourself Worthy for Everlasting Life." So, when the lawyer in Luke's gospel asked, "Lord, what must I do in order to gain eternal life?" you can almost feel Jesus rubbing his hands and glowing with excitement as he began to tell us how to prepare for the Big Day.

Since we all have gone to school, we know the difference between a good teacher and a bad one. (The good ones tell you what's going to be on the final exams—and they stick to it!) So let us exchange roles with the lawyer and ask Jesus the lawyer's question as though we were students and Jesus is our good teacher. Thinking of our finals, we say,

"Lord, what will be the questions asked on the Day of Judgment? We want to prepare ourselves for it. We want to do 'homework' in anticipation of things that will be covered on the test. Which parts of the world's importances must we be sure of to have a 'well done' record?"

Jesus thinks these are very good questions. His answer is summed up in a one-two punch. A double reference-of-love contains the whole law—love God and love others. That's it!

Then Jesus elaborates on each aspect of our responsibility. Jesus tells us we will be given a kind of essay question on "How Did Your Life Prove That You Loved God?" We will be given lots of time to write this essay question. We will reflect on how well we prayed to God and paid attention to his inspirations and learned his Scriptures. We will also report on how consistently we gave thanks to God by being faithful to religious observances.

This essay question will be only the first part of our finals. The other part will take even longer. We'll be given millions of true/false questions, covering every part of our lives, including people we have related to in any way—those we noticed or ignored, befriended or insulted, applauded or jeered at, were generous to or manipulated, loved or jilted, cared about or crossed off, were patient with or scolded, laughed with or laughed at—everyone, everywhere, every way, all our lives.

In Matthew's gospel (Chapter 25) Jesus speaks of the full scope of all those people who have come in and out of our lives. There are six sweeping categories. Jesus declares, "I consider it to have been done to me..." whenever we related to those who were:

1. Hungry (even hungry for attention, like children, or the elderly)

2. Thirsty (even thirsting for approval, like our school friends or coworkers)

3. Naked (those who are targets to fault-finders and gossips are "naked" to their enemies)

4. A Stranger (people who are feeble or who become disabled must adjust to new circumstances; they are "strangers" to the scary changes in their different life)

5. Sick (including those who may be physically healthy, but are sick at heart)

6. In prison (including those who are caught up in the prisons of depression, addiction, or any compulsive behavior)

Jesus will display this vast throng of needy people who have somehow, at some time, touched our lives. And he will say, "Did you care about them? Or did you neglect to care?"

The destiny of heaven or hell depends on which answer will prove to be the more prominent.

Our Lord's demand that we love others, and serve them in their various needs, is the same command in the gospels of both Matthew and Luke. But Matthew is a kind of spiritual Cecil B. DeMille—cosmic in scope—embracing a "cast of thousands." Everyone who has been cared for or neglected is included in this panorama.

Luke's gospel, in contrast, has a personal perspective. Here, Jesus focuses on what goes on inside the hearts and intentions of only three individuals.

The Parable of the Good Samaritan begins when the lawyer asks Jesus, "Who is my neighbor?" This was not a simple question. On the surface it just meant what it said. But underneath the words lay these inquiries: how far does the idea of "neighbor" stretch? must it include everybody? or may I be selective and refuse to love those I can't stand...or those my group dislikes?

Christ's response is the parable. He praised the Samaritan. It was he who proved himself a neighbor. It must have been a jolt for the audience, who were all Jews, to hear a Samaritan praised—a man who represented that despised and racially mistreated sub-group. Yet this individual was set up as the "Good Guy Who Deserves Heaven," while the (ordinarily respected) priest and Levite were presented as the "Neglecters of Love."

But there's more to this parable than just a command to stop being bigoted. The contemporaries of our Lord surely knew all the laws designed to guarantee religious purity. It was taboo for any priest or Levite to touch a corpse, even when the reasons for doing so were noble. If they did, they were forbidden to perform their works of ministry for a considerable length of time. They would lose their jobs, their salary, and their customary associations.

They knew that they'd be taking a big chance, as soon as they lifted up the poor guy who was badly beaten and thrown into the ditch. The man "looked half-dead." He might be dead by the time he was hoisted on the donkey and delivered to the innkeeper. The prudent thing was to weigh the consequences...and keep on their way, pretending they never saw the man at all. "We must be careful," was their thought. "We might lose our place within the priestly class; we might lose our livelihood for several years; and we might be strongly ridiculed by our friends for doing such a reckless thing just to help out a nobody!"

All this was part of the story behind the story of the Good Samaritan. The larger moral our Lord was making is much more demanding than it first appears to be. Jesus is telling us, "Look, I don't care what it will cost you in terms of energy or expense. I don't care if people laugh at you or criticize you for 'being a Good Samaritan.' Never mind any of those things. If you notice somebody who needs your love, you must reach out and give your love, no matter what the consequences. This is how you prove to me that you really do love your neighbor."

Prayer Setting

You are relaxed. Your mind has brought you to the most comfortable room you have ever known. It is early evening, the end of a perfect day. The fireplace is crackling with good noises, giving off a soft, peaceful glow. You are alone because you choose to be.

Think of some people you have helped during the last three years or so. Think of as many as you can. Remember how you encouraged them when they were steeped in their grief, or you assisted them financially, or drove them places, or shopped for them, or treated them to dinner...whatever. Consider these manifestations of your compassion and thoughtfulness as you go down memory lane.

Next step: imagine these people (and groups, too) sitting down in their own homes. They are writing thank-you notes to Jesus. In glowing terms, they tell him how much you have meant to them. Think of them smiling as they put into words how grateful they are for you.

Then they seal their letters and send them on to Jesus. Each is worded differently, of course. But they all tell Christ that on the whole, you are a decent and kind person. You were good to them. As far as they are concerned, you certainly have what it takes to gain everlasting life!

In the final scene, Jesus enters your comfortable room. He sits beside you. You watch the fire together for a while. Then he takes out those letters he has just received. He reads them all. Sometimes he chuckles...sometimes he says "Good!" out loud because of what he has just read. He puts a few of them in a special folder—the ones he likes best. And then he puts the letters on his lap and speaks to you with words like these...

Jesus Talks to You

My disciple, my friend, for the most part you have done me proud. I'm glad I died for you and sent you my Spirit and gave you my Church to grow you up good. Let me read you some of my favorite letters, mailed to me by people you have cared for, and listened to, and helped to renew their hope.

You will recognize some of the people and remember some of the situations. Others you have already forgotten. But they didn't forget. Listen to what they have to say:

(Imagine Jesus quoting from the letters he received. "Feel" the gentleness in his voice, as he brings these stories back to life. Sometimes he makes comments, adding to what has been written. Be attentive to the emphasis he gives to certain memories.

You may feel uncomfortable to hear such praise. Even so, accept it. The Lord's gratitude for your past kindness prepares you to do even better in the future. Let Jesus talk to you about this. Finally, at the end of your meditation, conclude with these prayers:)

You Pray to Jesus

Jesus, my Lord, I'm flabbergasted by this experience. My training always has been to think about what's wrong with me—how much I needed to shape up. So I expected the Last Judgment would force me to appear in front of a no-holds-barred courtroom to view a thousand hours of flashbacks displaying how I slipped up and sinned and neglected to be all that I could be.

I was kind of braced for that scene. Yet, here we are, the two of us, in easy chairs…with you reading testimonials from people who knew me when love and delightfulness were the experiences remembered.

It will be wonderful, Lord, if Judgment Day could be conducted this way. I want to think of these good stories more. I'm sure I won't get a big head—I'm too aware of my meanness and selfishness to think myself so perfect that I can sit in judgment on anybody else. No, I'm not good enough to do that!

Indeed, sometimes I've proven that I'm not very good at all. I sometimes get so frenzied by my own frustrations that I don't notice people who are hungry for attention or thirsting for approval or in the prisons of their compulsive behavior. Unlike the Good Samaritan, I'm sometimes so afraid of becoming "too drained" if I agree to help someone. I fail to love because of money worries and preoccupations with my own concerns, my own time.

Your Holy Spirit is what I need more of. Please help me, Lord, to put fresh energy into my desire to love others as you love them. I know I can do better, especially after this great evening of prayer we've had together.

Jesus, make sure I continue to measure up to your will-of-love. I hope that all the people in my future will be able to write you how I proved myself a good neighbor when they needed me.

You taught me—and I learned—what I must do in order to gain everlasting life. I did it. And I'm glad I did. And, when I get to heaven, I know I will be even gladder. Amen.

Chapter 20

Focusing on Found #2
(Luke 15–God Is a Good and Patient Shepherd)

A. This is what Jesus really said:

Jesus spoke to the Pharisees this parable:

What man among you, having 100 sheep, and losing one of them, does not leave the 99 in the desert and go after that which is lost, until he finds it? And when he has found it, he lays it on his shoulders, rejoicing. And on coming home, he calls together his friends and neighbors; and he says to them: "Rejoice with me because I found my sheep that was lost!"   —*Luke 15:1–6*

B. This is what Jesus did not say:

Jesus did not speak to anybody this parable:

What person among you, after losing one sheep, leaves the 99 in the custody of his family—ranting and raving that they darn well better not lose another one!—and goes off into the hills, wasting five hours tracking down the wayward sheep! When he finally finds the frightened creature, the shepherd shouts at him and unmercifully bawls him out with words like, "Do you see what hours of anguish I have gone through while you were out having a good time? Do you see my sandaled feet, all bruised and bleeding, all because of you! You are more trouble than all your brothers and sisters put together! You could have at least telephoned!"

And on and on goes the tirade until his voice runs out. Then the mean man drives the poor creature back ahead of him, mumbling all the time how these young animals are so irresponsible. When they get home, the sheep is locked up and the man goes to bed grumpy. And he would not speak to that truant sheep for a whole six months! This is not the gospel of the Lord!

Reflection

The second parable inserted above is only a "pretend story." It is ridiculous even to suggest that Jesus might have said it. But it is not make-believe as soon as we imagine that such words might have come from ourselves. Perhaps this "ugly parable" is the favorite way good people have to demonstrate their 30% mean side.

Idealism is the jumping off place for most "good people sins." Idealism is a wonderful motivator, but a terrible judge. The tendency to be idealistic often leads people into perfectionism. Then the demanding side of a perfectionist gets born...and this is what turns good people into scolds.

The mean shepherd in that "pretend story" was such a perfectionist. All he asked for was that everything, always, work out well! The cottage must run efficiently, all the time. The sheep must never fail to behave themselves—none of them must give him any worries or pester him when he is busy. If troubles do arise, watch out! Those who burst the bubble of Mr. Perfect's ideal world will get a tongue-lashing they deserve!

Of course, the man feels he is justified in his angry outbursts. "Who can blame me for losing my temper?" he will tell you. "Because of that blasted sheep, my energy was wasted—the whole afternoon got ruined and now I have bruises on my feet from going up and down those rugged hills in search of him!"

This is the way Mr. Perfect relates to people. Isn't it good that God does not treat us this way?

And isn't it good to be told how God does relate to us...in his "Good Shepherd-ly" way? Christ's parable is reassuring, especially when we realize how the shepherd in the parable must have gone to a lot of trouble on that long afternoon of searching, under the hot Palestinian sun. Probably the man did cut his feet on the rocks, and his clothes did get tangled up in the briar patches.

But Christ's version of the good shepherd does not show any scolding of the truant sheep. There were no harsh words, no "how could you do this to me" expressions. Nothing like that. The mood was joy, pure joy, because of what he found. It was not a playback of the misery endured because of what he lost.

When we operate out of the kind side of our nature, the virtue of compassion is instinctively in charge. We see people in need. We respond appropriately. We don't calculate the degree of hardship that might result once we let other people bite into our time. And we rejoice when good order is restored—when the "sheep" is found, the love rekindled, the friend reclaimed, the mess made right.

We can help ourselves get better by considering the "Good Shepherd" side of us. Tapping the memories of kind deeds done feeds us for future kindness. By drawing on past success, we can focus on more expansive possibilities.

Prayer Setting

In your imagination, go to your kitchen table. You are alone, waiting for Jesus to join you. Your window gives a lovely view of a hillside in Palestine. Watch, as a solitary shepherd moves about, down one valley, up another hill, searching for his lost sheep.

Pay attention, now, as you see that he found it. The poor thing was caught in a clump of underbrush that was strangling him. See the man free the little one, then put it on his shoulders. Then he dances a little dance—all smiles—as he begins to make his way home, where he will be the host of an impromptu celebration.

Let this scene remind you of occasions when similar experiences occurred in your life: a serious misunderstanding was resolved; wounds that had severed a friendship were healed; a serious mix-up in your job was straightened out; health came back after a painful illness; feuding members of your family patched things up, thanks to your gentle prodding; a marriage was restored; those who suffered from depression found a way to get hope back into their lives…

Remember these situations. And remember how grateful you were when things worked out so well. You didn't complain about how long it took before joy turned the corner. You didn't nag those people about "all the trouble they put you through." In those large, dramatic moments of your life, you concentrated on the happy out-come—not on the misery that was part of the "in-go"...

Jesus Talks to You

I'm glad you got so much practical meaning out of my Parable of the Good Shepherd. I must say it's always been one of my favorites.

What you were doing just now was meditating. You were thinking about how your life fit into the gospel passage. Good. Take these memories and let them be a "bank" against possible bitterness in the future. Continue to meditate on the "happy endings" that have been the best part of your life. Write them down (or develop them in your mind) as your personal versions of my parable.

After you've collected a few of them, come back to me and tell me your stories, just the way they really happened. I love stories, especially the ones about compassion and patience and celebrations at the end.

Just by bringing out the upbeat side of your past, you will be able to raise your self-image, which is sometimes dangerously low. And you will also be able to curb the tendency you sometimes have of criticizing other people when they don't come up to your standards.

Another advantage: by emphasizing the joy that came to you after your trials (in those "big events" of your life), you can better equip yourself to face the little everyday snags that frustrate your normal routine.

You see, my friend, it is easy to be like that Good Shepherd whenever you are going through a severe hardship, or an almost hopeless situation. On such occasions, where there is high drama and intense challenge, you have displayed a remarkable degree of endurance and resilience. All to your credit! But you must learn to have the same patience and good-natured understanding in the little challenges as well. When your family acts up, for instance; or when a friend is late; or when someone who promised to phone forgot to. Things like that.

Remember, I never related to people the way that grouchy shepherd scolded his lost sheep (in the "pretend parable"). I never nagged anyone—neither on big occasions nor during those small ordinary times when people proved themselves to be less than perfect.

Cross words and angry outbursts are not in my vocabulary. And they'd better not be in yours, either!

You Pray to Jesus

Fill me with your Spirit, Lord. I want to show my gratitude for the kindly way you've treated me, by doing the same for others. I want to be a searcher for what is lost, a patcher-up of what is torn or rifted, and a celebrator when health, happiness, and hopes revive.

I no longer want to be perfectionist-turned-scold. No. When people cause me grief or inconvenience, I'll just do what I can, working as best I can, in my flawed (sometimes quite frustrating) world.

Stories of my good shepherding are hints of yours, my Jesus. Let me understand it this way. Then I can look forward to the marvelous celebration we'll all enjoy in heaven…when you call us all together and tell us to:

"Rejoice with me,
for the friends I've made;
and the love that has returned
because of those who returned to me!"
Amen.

Chapter 21

Who's Wearing the Apron?
(*Luke 12, 17–How to Harness Moodiness*)

A. Jesus said to his disciples:
Blessed are those servants whom the master, on his return, shall find waiting...and working...and giving the household their ration of grain, regularly...I solemnly assure you, the master will put on his apron and make the servants recline at table and he will serve them. —*Luke 12:35–43*

B. Jesus said to his disciples:
If one of you had a servant [doing his day's work] and he then came in from the field, would you say to your servant, "Come at once and recline at table while I serve you"? Would you not say, instead, "Prepare my supper; put on your apron and serve me until I have dined; you may eat and drink afterward!" Does the master thank his servant for doing his day's work? I do not think so. It is the very same with you. When you have done everything that is commanded of you, you must say, "We are ordinary servants; we have done no more than our duty." —*Luke 17:7–11*

Reflection
You could call this chapter a consideration of "Apron, Apron, Who's Got the Apron?" In the first parable, Jesus depicts a wonderful scene that will happen afterward. When we have finished with this life, Jesus will engage us in an ultimate review. He will tally up all the times we have been good to people. He will make note of all the occasions when we have worked for others, served them in their needs,

responded to their appeals...whenever we have healed and helped, listened and loved.

At first it will be a personal interview, you and the Lord. Then, when the intimate scene is concluded, he will assemble all the heavenly court in the Great Hall. The Lord will open a large scroll and declare your lifetime-full of deeds. Using a celestial loudspeaker (and with a band that flourishes drum rolls now and then) Jesus will broadcast your biography to one and all:

"Whereas _____ (your name), on such and such a date, did perform this act of love, that deed of kindness, for this and that individual... Therefore, he/she is someone after my own heart, and deserves to be rewarded. (Drum roll...)

"And whereas... (Jesus tells the particulars of the next time you were "found working and giving people-in-need your love"...)

"And whereas... (This is the way it continues until your life on earth is "wrapped up.")"

It might seem that the final roll call will go on for a very long time. No matter. Eternity will last forever. Besides, time as we know it, no longer exists. In heaven, it will be impossible to get bored or "antsy."

Finally, after Jesus has praised you for each particular proof of your patience under trials, your love for others, your positive achievements of all kinds...Jesus will conduct you to a splendid dining room. He will sit you down at table...and then (marvel of marvels!) the Lord himself will put on an apron and wait on you!

Made special in front of everybody! Welcomed by Blessed Mary and all the saints! Enjoying festivities that will last forever! Served by Jesus, with his apron on! Now won't that be wonderful!

Prayer Setting

Recall at least three occasions when you proved loyal to Christ and to his principles of love. Also remember three times when you endured hardships or sickness without undue complaining. Then list three other times when you cared for someone in ways that made a noticeable difference in their lives.

Let your mind dwell on these categories for a while. Do not link them to any "killer phrases" that you sometimes say—things like

"Yes, I did good, but I could have done better!" or "Yes, I helped others, so where did it get me?" or "So why didn't they thank me?"

Resist saying such words. Try to resist even having the thoughts. Just repeat to yourself, "I saw an opportunity to do good, so I did it. And I'm glad I did." Period! On other occasions, say to yourself, "I suffered from such-and-such a distress; but I made the best of those bad situations and did not make a nuisance of myself." Period!

Stay with these thoughts for a while. Then imagine being given your "Day of Appreciation" as Jesus has already suggested it will happen. See yourself sitting down at the head of a large table. Take all the time you need to place your friends close to you. Also at your table are all the members of your family and the special saints you have loved...whoever comes to mind in this prayer-image.

Then observe Jesus, as he solemnly puts on his apron. He makes sure you are all comfortable. He calls you blessed once again. He commands happiness to be always at your side. Then he serves you—all of you—to your hearts' content.

Remain with this amazing scenario, promised by the Lord himself, as long as you possibly can...

Jesus Talks to You

My friend, return to that scene every now and then. It will help you, especially when you are discouraged by lack of success—when life seems flat and you get frustrated—and when you tend to get down on others because you are down on yourself. Remember that I am ready to put my apron on and serve you in the festive hall of heaven.

But remember, too, there is another apron to be concerned about—the "While I'm Still Living on Earth Apron," mentioned in Luke's 17th chapter.

It is the one you must put on—and keep on—until the day you die. And every time you are feeling uppity, or proud, or full of demands that other people should appreciate you, or full of self-pity when they don't, remember who is wearing the apron.

Whenever you have given in to your horrible moodiness, you have done so because you were mixed up about the aprons. You formed a misconception concerning who ought to be serving whom. Almost all of the sins of the good people are infected by one cancer—the demand that other people should serve them, because of some past favors done, or because of some pressing needs they have. Good people can rot the good they do when they want to be rewarded by God and treated by humans with signs of appreciation and the comfort of "everybody dropping everything" to take care of them.

Sometimes, when these demands aren't met, good people can get so angry at God, they will quit on him. And they can get so angry at others they cry outrage against the unfairness of it all. Or (the worst reaction) they sulk and mope and refuse to be happy with anybody... and act out all those songs that complain about their "achy-breaky heart":

"All my friends are knocking at my door.
They've asked me to go out
a hundred times or more.
But then I say that I prefer my gloom!
And here I'll stay
inside my lonely room...."

Moans and groans like that!

Don't get me wrong, my disciple, my friend. I can't blame you for feeling bad when you are rejected, or jilted, or unloved, or unappreciated. I wept when the people of Jerusalem rejected me. I felt very sad when Judas betrayed me. And it really hurt because all those thousands I had helped and healed never came around to be on my side when the authorities rigged the crowd to call out for my crucifixion.

Sure, I grieved. Real tears. But I didn't stop loving. That's the point. I never took my apron off. I said to myself, "Okay, the facts are that many people have rebuked me and don't like me anymore. But there is still Mary, my mother. There are still my disciples who will soon come back to the upper room and wait for me. And there is you. Yes, you. I knew there would be you two thousand years ago—you and all those countless others who would prove faithful to me throughout the centuries."

With these thoughts to sustain me, I continued. Three days later, as you know, I conquered death and rose to my place in heaven. I am proud of my wounds, suffered because I loved you. I had the power to rescue all people from the finality of death and from every other thing that puts happiness out of reach. And so I did it.

Heaven is your destiny, as well. It is my gift to you. In your present world, you do feel battered, sometimes. Things will happen that will cause you to feel used, taken for granted, rejected by people you counted on. Never mind. You still must live my way. Don't expect to be served with rewards or appreciation. When such gratuities do come to you, fine. Enjoy them. But if the return of thoughtfulness is not given you, don't sulk or mope or quit on life.

As long as you remain on earth, it is you who has the apron on. Only afterward, in heaven, will the roles be changed: when I will escort you to your place, and praise you to the vast assembly, and put my apron on, and wait on you.

You Pray to Jesus

Dear Jesus, help me to really understand the most earnest appeal you made to us—that we must never get discouraged. Let me never forget you, who created me and equipped me with all that was necessary to live out my destiny.

You gave me my apron and told me to keep it on. Let me love others (and myself) according to the gifts I have…and according to the opportunities that seem to keep popping up in my life. Teach me how to survive the aftereffects of my own goodness. Let me not ruin my kindnesses by demanding that I should be rewarded later on…as if all those I have helped should put their apron on and wait on me!

Make sure, my Lord, that I never again yield to the seductive lure of self-pity. Even after a whole lifetime of loving service, I want to say, "No big deal! I was simply loving others, in my small way, after the pattern of how you so largely loved me first."

Let me keep my apron handy and wear it more often than I'd like to. After all, my Lord, you came to serve us, not to be served by us. You loved, whether you were loved back or not. The drum rolls and the big appreciation party will come later on. Right now, I've got work to do. Amen.

Chapter 22

Having a Hint of Heaven
(John 16–What Will It Feel Like to Be Really Happy?)

A. Jesus spoke to the people in parables, saying:
The kingdom of heaven is like a king who made a marriage feast
for his son...and he said, "The marriage feast indeed is ready...
Go to the crossroads and invite to the marriage feast whomever
you shall find." Then his servants went out into the roads and
gathered all whom they found—both bad and good. And the
wedding feast was filled with guests. Now the king went in to
see the guests and he saw that there were some who did not
have on a wedding garment. And he said to them, "Friends, how
is it that you came in here without a wedding garment?" But
they said not a word. Then the king said to the attendants, "Bind
their hands and their feet and cast them forth into the darkness
outside..."   —*Matthew 22:1–13*

B. Jesus said [his last parable] to his disciples:
Do not let your hearts be troubled. Do not be afraid. I go away
to prepare a place for you. A woman about to give birth is sorrowful, because her hour has come. But when she has brought
forth her child, joy makes her forget her anguish because life
has come into the world. So I shall see you again...and your
hearts will rejoice, and your joy no one will take away from you.
—*John 16:1–20*

Reflection #1 (*Considering our Entrance into Heaven*)
Christ's parable of the "Feast Inside/Darkness Outside" explains,
very dramatically, the contrast between love and hate, heaven and
hell, God and grudges.

Jesus consistently reveals two truths that appear to be contradictory. Revelation #1: God is love. God extended his goodness by creating us; then he recreated us in the life of his own Son. He does not condemn; he saves. He desires that love and life abound, never-endingly.

Revelation #2: Hell is real; and people (somehow) live there. Jesus warned us not to imagine how dismal that place is. All we know it to be is a "forever locality," absolutely devoid of love or hope and any kind of benevolent fellow-feeling. It is useless to joke about that place. We cannot say, "At least, in hell, all my friends will be there! Ha, ha, ha!" There will be no such things as friends—or friendliness—in hell.

How, then, can these two truths match up? God is love. He does not send anyone to hell. Yet hell is terribly real, with real people in it. How can both statements be true?

The answer lies in Christ's parable. God's unconditional cordiality shows through, as the story unfolds. When it is discovered that there is still room in the Banquet Hall of Heaven, messengers are commissioned to go out and bring in all people, from all ages, from every highway and hedgerow and back alley that ever existed—"and make them come in!"

So, in we come—you and I and everybody else. Jesus says that "people both good and bad" are given a royal welcome. That telling phrase does not mean that the "good people" march through the main gate to the Grand Affair, while the "bad ones" sneak in by the side door.

No. Jesus is speaking about the theme of this book. We humans—every one of us—are a mix of good and bad. We sometimes operate from the kind side of our personalities; and we sometimes exhibit our mean streak. We are 70% good, 30% bad (or some blend of fractions thereof).

Once we admit this composite of our personality, we all enter the one gate, are warmly welcomed, and then directed to the side room where we will be fitted with our wedding garment.

But, as the story unfolds, something strange happens to a minority of the guests. God mixes in with the crowd and discovers that some people (over there in the corner) are not wearing their wedding garments, and he asks them, "Why not?" But they stay sulking, refusing to say a word!

We cannot interpret this interchange in such a way that we feel sorry for those improperly dressed. We can't say, "Too bad they were excluded, just because they couldn't afford to rent a tuxedo!"

No, that was not the case. Jesus was referring to the marriage customs of his culture. At that time, a more than ample supply of garments was available in the vestibule. They were long white robes, reaching to the ankles, shaped something like the robes choir members wear. All they had to do was put on one that fit. As soon as they did so, their attire declared to all the vast assembly, "This shows you how I gladly take part in the celebration. I join in everybody's joy. I am very happy to be with all of you!"

That will be the statement made. And that will be precisely the declaration that "has to be rejected" by those who are determined to abide nowhere but hell.

From Christ's parable, we conclude that the place outside "where there is snarling and the gnashing of teeth" is populated by people who have condemned themselves. God does not cast them forth. God simply allows their bitterness to continue for all eternity.

Some people will unceasingly insist that they cannot take part in any joyful occasion where "those people" are present…or where they would have to rub shoulders with "that person who treated me so cruelly!" Heaven is a place that is locked into certain unchangeable conditions. The greatest of these conditions is unconditional forgiveness of all wrongdoers. And this is precisely the one condition that grudge-keepers cannot live with.

So what can God do? Must divine love stoop to human bigotry? Or held grudges? Or spiteful vengeance? No way! Never! If we reject God's standards of acceptance into heaven—absolute forgiveness and unconditional love—there is nowhere to go but out…out into the darkness of eternity's outside.

Guided Imagery Prayer

Pretend that you have just died. Gradually, you understand that you have come to a place of peace, in an atmosphere that sings of the harmony of all creation. Then a message reaches your ears: soon, everyone who died that day will be formally welcomed into paradise. The festivities will start in an hour. You'll be told where to get your festive garment and when to join God in the Great Hall. In the meantime, you're urged to stroll around and renew old friendships.

You must mix in—that's part of the initiation. But, as you walk around, you notice people of different racial and ethnic backgrounds, a culturally diverse group, all sizes and shapes, backgrounds and histories.

Then you see those who used to fill you with disgust because of their politics, or their language, or their hairdo, or customs of behavior, or style of clothes, or age, or choice of music...or...or... Your list seems endless. Well, there they are—waiting for you to show some sign that you will finally accept them.

Next, you meet certain individuals you can't stand. They hurt you deeply. They were terribly unfair to you, or they cruelly mistreated someone you loved. Up to your deathbed, you never forgot—or forgave—what they did. You hated them. Hated them! Well, there they are, waiting for you to show some sign that you have finally relented in your wrath. (The party will go on without you, remember, unless you agree to be reconciled.)

You feel so bad about all these peacemaking conditions that you go to the corner and sulk. You reject the festive garment when it is handed to you. Then (as he does in the parable) God comes over to you, puts his arm around you and begs you to change your heart:

Please, my friend, please don't insist on showing a long face on such a joyous occasion. Look all around you. See the peace and serenity of my paradise.

Don't throw it all away because my Son chose to love and forgive the sins of those who treated you so shamelessly. This is a different place, this heaven of mine. Here is an atmosphere of complete acceptance. Don't let your perceived or remembered hurts prevent you from living up to all the goodness I want to give you. I want you to be happy, forever. But this happiness must be on my terms, not yours.

When my Son died on the cross, he used his last breath to beg me to forgive sinners. So I did. And here they are: forgiven. You must forgive them, also. In heaven, we have brand new ways for getting along with others. They weren't available on earth; here, they are. Trust me.

"Let go of your prejudices, your bitter feelings. Put on the garment of festivity and let's enter the Great Hall together. Just as my Son has promised, we'll both have a wonderful time!"

Reflection #2 (*Considering Heaven Itself, Once We Get Used to It*)

We know more about what heaven isn't, than what it is. When the Sadducees challenged Jesus on the subject, they presented the case of a woman who successively married seven brothers. They asked, mockingly, "Master, when this woman gets to heaven, whose wife will she be? For she married all seven!" (You can almost see their faces framed in smirks; you can almost hear them saying "Nyah, nyah," like children teasing another child!)

Jesus rebuked them severely. "Be quiet! You cannot imagine what it is like to live the life-style of angels. Don't try to toy with concepts which are far beyond your capacity to comprehend!" (Matthew 22:23–33; Mark 12:18; Luke 20:27–40). St. Paul, too, shuts down all fantasies about the afterlife: "Some people wonder, 'How will the dead be raised up? What kind of body will we have?' These are silly and stupid questions! The seed you sow in the ground does not know what the full-grown plant will be until it dies first and then grows into its new life" (1 Cor 15:35).

We shouldn't be surprised that Jesus refused to give any details about what heaven will be like. First graders understand that they can't satisfactorily explain to their three-year-old brothers or sisters what life will be like once they get to first grade.

And no adult is able to explain to a first-grader what the joys of an adult are. Tell a seven-year-old about the good feelings you have when you sit with a friend, hour after hour, or listen to your favorite music, or enjoy the opera or a show, or finally solve a problem you've been working on all week. Try to convince a child the joy these experiences give you, and you will be met by a quizzical gaze and words like "What! No video games? No skateboards? No burgers and fries? How could you have any fun?"

You would be reduced to a shrug of the shoulders and a rather unsatisfactory response: "Well, kid, there's nothing I can say that will help you much. You'll just have to grow up first, before you can understand."

Jesus said about the same words to the Sadducees (and to us all): "You cannot understand what heaven will be like. You can't even have a picture of it! Don't try. You'll just have to wait until you get there."

There's more to Christ's revelation, though. Jesus didn't just tell us to "Be quiet and wait for it!" In the last parable he ever spoke, he gave us a beautiful hint of heaven's "life-style." It is recorded in John's gospel. On Holy Thursday, at the very end of his long discourse where Jesus tried so valiantly to encourage his woebegone apostles, he promised that he would be like a mother giving birth to her child. He revealed that the suffering of Good Friday would be like his "child-birth pangs"; and then, on Easter, he would bring us forth into the place he had prepared for us, a place where nothing, and no one, will ever take our joy away.

This will happen because Christ said it will happen. We will experience such a quantum leap of living that the phenomenon can only be compared to the difference between the cramped way babies live in their mothers' wombs and the free life-style they have after they are born and grow up and enter all the capacities for happiness that adults possess.

Imagine this scene: There you are, beside a pregnant woman, talking into her stomach area. Make believe that you are having a conversation with the little baby inside. Pretend the baby can understand what you are saying. You begin: "Hey kid, I bet you can't wait until you get out of that place, right? I bet you're counting the days before you will be free to walk by yourself and swing in trees and splash mud puddles and feel the sun in your face and have friends and tell jokes and watch TV and everything. I bet you're really looking forward to living this way, right?"

Well, if the child could understand, and could speak, he would say, "What is this weirdo talking about?! There are no such thing as trees! What is the sun? What are jokes? What are mud puddles? All of this is absolutely incomprehensible. They don't exist. They can't exist!"

And then you would have to say, "Sorry, kid. You're going to have to die to your style of life in your mother's womb, first. You'll have to say goodbye to what you once were, before you can live in a world that has trees and sun and jokes and friends and mud puddles...and all kinds of unimaginably good stuff in it."

Guided Imagery Prayer

Try to remember the moment you were born. You probably can't, but you know you did cry when the umbilical cord was cut. You were very fearful and full of misgivings because you had just died to the only world you knew... and you didn't know (as yet) how you would manage in the scary world you were pushed into. Now, though, you are glad that life changed from the "womb world" to the one you've grown accustomed to.

On the day you die, you will experience a quantum leap even greater than the first one, when Jesus brings you into the world he has prepared for you. There is no sense in trying to conceive how this will happen, or what will come of it. You can't foresee that life-style any more than you could imagine what this world would be like when you were inside your mother.

All you have to go on is Christ's promise—you will live a way of life that far exceeds your ability to comprehend. You will experience an awesome sense of happiness. It will be both immediate and everlasting; always new, yet never dulled; spontaneously impulsive in its beauty, yet as comfortably consoling as an old pair of slippers. And it will be a joy (Christ's words) that nobody, and nothing, will take away from you.

This is what Jesus said—this and no more. We know he will keep his promise. He will reconnect us to everything that has given us happiness here on earth. We—somehow—will still enjoy there what we have enjoyed here. (Just because we cannot imagine how this will happen, does not mean that it won't happen.)

Christ's promise of everlasting happiness is the greatest pledge of all. It's worth waiting for, and working for. Jesus will take away our tears, and put us in a perfect place: "When he will see us again; and our hearts will rejoice and our joy will be God's gift to us, forever."

Afterword

A final prayer to Mary: Blessed Mary, keep me in your care. You are the best example of how to respond to God's invitation. You simply said, "Okay," when God wanted you to join him in his Plan of Love. You didn't hesitate, or hedge, or ask questions. You just said, "Let it be done to me, as you wish." And so it happened. And it all worked out so well!

Give me your trusting spirit, my Lady. When I get near to death, let me "let it be" in the same way. I don't want to second-guess God's all-inclusive love, or make things difficult because of my remembered grudges or the hurts I've held on to. I want to allow your son to bring me to birth into his world of perfect happiness. And I want it to happen his way.

Be with me, Blessed Mother, at the hour of my death. And pray that I may be always open to surprises, always available for love. Amen.

For your personal prayers and reflections

_____

_____

_____

_____

_____

_____

_____

_____

_____

_____

_____

_____

_____

_____

_____

For your personal prayers and reflections

Other Books by Isaias Powers...

Healing Words from Jesus

This unique book helps us recognize and clear away the obstacles that prevent Christ's healing powers from working. This book will go far to nourish spiritual growth and shows how to develop a closer relationship to Jesus. ISBN: 0-89622-682-4, 152 pp, $7.95

Healing Words from Mary

Entering the Mysteries of the Rosary

Father Ike helps Marian devotees open up a prayer conversation with the Blessed Mother and use her inspiration to pray for themselves and for others. Using the mysteries of the rosary, he helps readers examine their own thoughts, feelings, and emotions in order to find solace, understanding, and inspiration.

ISBN: 0-89622-702-2, 96 pages, $7.95

Quiet Places With Jesus

Fr. Powers guides readers to discover how Jesus understands their human joys and sorrows and how to cope with difficult times. A helpful appendix leads readers to the pages that will address particular needs or issues.

ISBN: 0-89622-086-9, 128 pp, $7.95 (order B-17)

Audiobook: Three 60-minute cassettes, print material, $24.95 (order A-31)

Letters from an Understanding Friend

These "letters from Jesus" are so helpful when we are looking for someone with whom to share our problems, fears, and feelings. The understanding in this book is intimate and healing. Great for personal reading and for gift-giving. ISBN: 0-89622-413-9, 96 pp, $7.95

Available at religious bookstores or from:

TWENTY-THIRD PUBLICATIONS
P.O. Box 180 • Mystic, CT 06355

1-800-321-0411
E-Mail:ttpubs@aol.com